THE KING ARTHUR ILLUSTRATED GUIDE

THE
KING ARTHUR
ILLUSTRATED
GUIDE

by
R.J. HUTCHINGS

DYLLANSOW TRURAN

3

Published by Dyllansow Truran.
Trewolsta, Trewirgie, Redruth, Cornwall.
© 1983 Richard J. Hutchings

ISBN 0 097566 50 2

Reprinted 1989

Printed and bound in Great Britain by
Short Run Press Ltd., Exeter

PREFACE

In this booklet I have attempted to sketch the growth of Arthurian legends from the twelfth-century biography of Geoffrey of Monmouth to the nineteenth-century *Idylls of the King* by the poet Alfred Tennyson. With the aid of illustrations, moreover, I have set out to guide readers to the places associated most closely with Arthur's life, at the same time separating - as far as that is possible - the historical from the legendary King. Attention has been focussed on Geoffrey, Sir Thomas Malory and Tennyson because of all other British writers these have contributed most to Arthurian literature.

R.J.H. 1982

By the same Author:

Idylls of Farringford - Alfred Tennyson (Brodies)
Landfalls of the Romantic Poets
Dickens on an Island
King of the Mystics - Robert Browning
Tennyson: Selected Poetry (Brodies/Pan Books)
The Wordsworth Poetical Guide to the Lakes (Hunnyhill publications)
West Country Poems of Wordsworth & Coleridge
An Island of Poetry (Saunders)
Isle of Wight Literary Haunts

© Richard J. Hutchings, 1982

ACKNOWLEDGEMENTS

The topographical material in this booklet is based mainly on the place-names in the legendary *History of the Kings of Britain,* by Geoffrey of Monmouth, and on Sir Thomas Malory's *Le Morte d'Arthur.* I should like to thank Dr. Bella Millett of the Department of English, The University, Southampton, for sparing time to read through the script critically; also my wife Elizabeth, for her opinions and advice on it.

My gratitude to Mr. F.E. Gibson of St. Mary's, Isles of Scilly, the Hampshire County Council, the Hampshire Record Office and the Winchester City Museum for permission to reproduce illustrations in this booklet. Other photographs are by my son Keith and by myself.

My gratitude, also, to editors, publishers and translators of the books listed in Further Reading at the end of this book, pp. 88, 89.

THE KING ARTHUR ILLUSTRATED GUIDE

CONTENTS

ILLUSTRATIONS

PROLOGUE

The old world knows not his peer, nor will the future show us his equal: he alone towers over other kings, better than the past ones and greater than those that are to be.

-Joseph of Exeter (fl. 1190)

A man clearly not to be dreamed of in fallacious fables, but to be proclaimed in veracious histories, as one who long sustained his tottering country, and gave the shattered minds of his fellow-citizens an edge of war.

- William of Malmesbury (1125)

She that is oppressed shall at last prevail, and shall resist the fierceness of the strangers. For the Boar of Cornwall (Arthur) shall bring succour and shall trample their necks beneath his feet. The islands of the ocean shall be subdued to his power and he shall possess the forests of Gaul. The house of Romulus shall dread his fierceness, and his end shall be doubtful. In the mouth of the peoples shall he be celebrated, and his deeds shall be food unto the tellers of tales.

- Geoffrey of Monmouth, The Prophecies of Merlin (1148)

Arthur was a young man only fifteen years old; but he was of outstanding courage and generosity, and his inborn goodness gave him such grace that he was loved by almost all the people......

- Geoffrey of Monmouth, History of the Kings of Britain (c. 1136)

Arthur fought the Saxons alongside the kings of the Britons, but he himself was the leader in the battles (dux bellorum)......

- Nennius (died c. 811), The History of Britain

Arthur never heard speak of a knight in praise, but he caused him to be numbered of his household. Arthur made the Round Table, so reputed of the Britons.

- Wace of Jersey, Li Romans de Brut (1155)

...... I will fare to Avalun, to the fairest of all maidens, to Argante the

Queen, and elf most fair, and she shall make my wounds all sound; make me all whole with healing draughts. And afterwards I will come to my kingdom, and dwell with the Britons with mickle joy.

- Layamon's Brut (c. 1190)

Presently (the Saxons') pride was checked for a while through the great Arthur, King of the Britons. They were largely cleared from the island and reduced to subjection. But when this same Arthur, after many victories which he won gloriously in Britain and Gaul, was summoned at last from human activity, the way was open for the Saxons to go again into the island, and there was great oppression of the Britons, destruction of churches and persecution of saints. This persecution went on through the times of many kings, Saxons and Britons, striving back and forth.....

- 'William' writing on the Legend of St. Goeznovius
in the 11th century.

THE HISTORICAL ARTHUR

If there was ever an historical King Arthur, he lived most probably in the Dark Ages of the fifth and sixth centuries. The Imperial Roman Legions had returned home in 410, leaving his country entirely at the mercy of the brutal invading hordes of Saxons, Angles, Jutes and Picts. Systematically they proceeded to smash the last vestiges of Roman civilisation in Britain, pillaging and ruthlessly putting men, women and children to the sword. Few lived to tell the tale.

It is believed that in 418 a last attempt by Roman Legions was made to reoccupy parts of Britain in a rescue mission, but the Roman Empire itself was crumbling fast and could ill-afford to spare men on such a punitive expedition.

Since 418 British society and the economy (a familiar tale) had begun to decline. In 425 Vortigern, a new leader, rose to prominence, but could do little to stem the tide of the invaders. Pagan raids began in earnest in 440 and ten years later there were enemy settlements in Thanet and the surrounding areas, at Vortigern's invitation. His intention in inviting Saxons to Britain had been, firstly, to discourage their raids, and secondly, to employ them to protect Britain against the onslaughts of the Picts, Scots and Irish, who attacked from Scotland and West Wales.

But the Saxons outwitted Vortigern by inviting thousands of their fellow-countrymen to join them. In 457 the Anglo-Saxons rebelled against their paymaster, and proceeded to lay waste the lowlands of Britain. The inhabitants fled to Armorica (Brittany) in their thousands. Vortigern died c. 461 and succeeding him came Ambrosius Aurelianus, a survivor of Roman society who had lived unmolested in the West Country. Employing Roman cavalry tactics he rallied the British under him and somehow managed to provide a respite temporarily from enemy incursions; and by the end of AD. 470, they mounted a counter-offensive against the Anglo-Saxons. But the enemy still occupied the east, south-east and south of the country, and British emigration to Armorica continued.

Ambrosius Aurelianus led his cavalry into a battle at Badon Hill (believed to be a hill near Bath). Sometime during the battle he died, and it seems that Arthur, then a young man, took over command and totally defeated the enemy, driving them out of the Thames valley, leaving only peaceful settlements in the east.

The historian, Nennius, wrote *Historia Brittonum* while living in Brecknock and Radnor, and in it he chronicled a list of Arthur's twelve victories. The problem seems to be that not all of the names he mentions can be identified, though numerous attempts to do so have been made.

Arthur's Twelve Victories: (from *Historia Brittonum,* 9th century)

1. At Glein. 2,3,4,5, at Dublas in the region of Linnuis (Lincoln?). 6. On the River Bassas. 7. In the wood of Celidon (Caledonia). 8. By Castle Guinnion in which Arthur 'carried on his shoulders an image of St. Mary Ever-Virgin, and there was great slaughter of them, through the strength of Our Lord Jesus Christ and of the Holy Mary his maiden-mother.' 9. In the City of the Legion (Caerleon?). 10. On the bank of the River Tribruit. 11. On the hill called Agned. 12. On Mount Badon, 'in which - on that one day - there fell in one slaughter of Arthur's, nine hundred and sixty men; and none slew them but he alone, and in all his battles he remained victor.'

Two of Arthur's battles are mentioned in the Welsh Annals:

516 AD - The battle of Badon, in which Arthur carried the Cross of our Lord Jesus Christ for three days and three nights on his shoulders (for shoulders read shield) and the Britons were victors.

537 AD - The Battle of Camlann, in which Arthur and Medraut fell: and there was plague in Britain and Ireland.

MOUNT BADON - BATH?

Bath seems the most likely site for his greatest battle, though other sites, such as Liddington castle, near Swindon, or Baydon Hill or Badbury Rings have been suggested as alternatives.

According to Geoffrey of Monmouth, after Arthur's army had soundly defeated the Saxons in the north, the enemy promised to return to their own country and to leave Britain in peace. However, after they had set sail from our shores, they turned south round our coasts to Torbay, where they landed and advanced into the West Country, marauding as they went.

Arthur hurried south to deal with his treacherous foes and encountered them at Bath where they were encamped on Mount Badon. The army had no alternative but to attack the enemy in his advantageous position, fighting its way up the slopes. But the battle did not go well at first, and many of the men were slaughtered. Arthur was roused to fury. As always in battle he wore a leather jerkin, and on his head a gold helmet with a crest carved in the shape of a dragon. He protected himself from the relentless blows of the enemy's broad-swords and lances with a circular shield called *Pridwen* which was adorned with the likeness of the Blessed Mary, Mother of God. At his side hung the 'peerless sword, Caliburn (Excalibur), which was forged in the Isle of Avalon', and in his right hand he bore a spear called *Ron,* which was 'long, broad in the blade and thirsty for slaughter'. Thus armed, he rallied his men to the terrible task ahead of them.

Arthur advanced at the head of his men, and as he climbed the slopes of Mount Badon he cut a swathe of death throught the Saxon soldiery, killing 470 in all. Emboldened by their king's superhuman strength and courage, his followers copied his example and soon routed the enemy, bringing peace to Britain for many years.

The earliest allusion to Arthur being a 'king' is in the Breton *Legend of St. Goeznovius* (c. 1019). When Britons fled to Brittany before the invading Saxons in the 5th century, Arthur was remembered as 'the great king of the Britons'.

In the twelfth-century *Life of St. Padarn,* the king was referred to as 'a certain *tyrannus* by the name of Arthur'; *tyrannus,* meaning, in this sense, an uninherited kingship. Arthur is said to have broken into Padarn's cell and taken a treasured tunic which a Jerusalem patriarch had given him. Whereupon the earth opened up and entrapped him to the neck. He was only allowed to escape after apologising to the monk.

HISTORICAL TINTAGEL

The battles listed in the Welsh Annals and in Nennius's Chronicles are all that are known about the life of Arthur. We do not even know if in fact he was a king, but just a *dux bellorum,* a warlord, who led sections of the British army into battle against the Saxons. As for the place of his birth, nothing is known, and in no way is he connected with Tintagel except in the *History* of Geoffrey of Monmouth which is largely fiction.

There is evidence however of there having been a Dark Age community living in Tintagel's famous headland, where pottery of the period had been found. There, too, are the remains of a Celtic monastery on the plateau, and lower down, a twelfth-century castle built by Reginald, Earl of Cornwall about the time that Geoffrey was writing the first biography of Arthur, in which he asserts that Tintagel was his birth-place.

TINTAGEL - ARTHUR'S LEGENDARY BIRTHPLACE

King Arthur was the legendary son of Uther Pendragon and Ygerna, wife of Gorlois, Duke of Cornwall, and was born about 475 AD at Tintagel Castle in Cornwall. His first biography, upon which our story is based, was by Geoffrey of Monmouth, bishop of Llandaff, who lived from 1100 to 1154. Because his *History of the Kings of Britain* was so factually unreliable, Geoffrey has been called the father of British fiction. Unfortunately we have little other evidence of Arthur's life to draw on and must be content with what Geoffrey told us about the circumstances of his birth.

King Uther was desperately in love with Ygerna. One Easter the king

13

ordered a feast to be held to which many Princes and Knights were invited. Among them was Gorlois, Duke of Cornwall, and his wife Ygerna. Her beauty quite overwhelmed Uther who unashamedly made known his feelings toward her during the celebrations and feasting, sending Gorlois into a jealous rage. Acting on impulse the duke dragged away his wife from the festivities without so much as a by-your-leave to the king, his host. Together they fled to Tintagel, Ygerna to be secured in the castle on the peninsula and he to a nearby fort to divert Uther's attention should he follow.

Determined that his passionate love for Ygerna should not be thwarted, King Uther assembled an army and went in pursuit of the fleeing couple. Warned of their coming, Gorlois prepared his small army to engage Uther's much larger forces. Inevitably Uther laid siege to the fort, but during the engagement he consulted Merlin, the magician and mentor, as how best to gain access to Tintagel Castle. It was known that three men could, by virtue of its inaccessibility, defend the castle against a whole army.

Merlin used his magic to make Uther look like Gorlois, and the King thereby gained access to the interior and to Ygerna's bed-chamber where Arthur was conceived. Duke Gorlois was killed in battle, and under duress Ygerna accepted Uther as her husband thus legalising the union and providing an heir to the throne to lead the British against the threatening Saxon forces. But Uther died of sickness before Arthur's birth, believing he had failed in his duty to his country.

HIS YOUTH AT DUNSTER

It is said that as soon as Arthur had been weaned by his mother, he was taken to foster parents by Merlin, to be educated and prepared for his regal duties, and that he lived, either at Celliwic, near Padstow in Cornwall, or at Dunster (Dindraethou) in Somerset, where he was taught the martial arts. If the latter is correct, he would have been under the tutelage of Prince Cadwy, who ruled there.

KING ARTHUR'S CORONATION AT SILCHESTER, HAMPSHIRE

Arthur was crowned King at Silchester by Dubricius, Archbishop of the City of the Legions (Caerleon or Chester) when he was a fifteen-year-old boy. From Silchester, called Calleva Atrebatum by the Romans, roads radiated to London, Chichester, Winchester, Old Sarum, Cirencester, and the West, to Dorchester, and Alchester and Watling Street. Silchester was the capital city of the government district known as Civitas Atrebatum. Calleva Atrebatum means 'the woodland town of the Atrebates,' then situated in the forest of

Pamber. A few miles north of Basingstoke, it is near the A34. The Roman walls enclose 107 acres of prime arable land on the property of Manor Farm, and when the crops are ripe, the grid-iron street patterns become visible from the air. Calleva Atrebates was built by a Belgic tribe from Arras, who settled south of the Thames after the conquest of Gaul by the Romans in 57 BC. Another Gallic tribe, the Catuvellauni, settled north of the Thames. But in time they infiltrated south and absorbed their Gallic brethren into their own population. Their leader was Cunobellinus, known more familiarly as Cymbeline, and characterised by Shakespeare in one of his plays. Calleva was built about ten years after the birth of Christ.

When the Romans occupied Calleva, in their obsession with orderliness they planned and constructed a grid-iron system of roads and streets between AD90 and 130. The town then had a population of about 4000, and at its centre was the Forum, Basilica & Baths beside a stream flowing out through the east wall near the church of St. Mary and Manor Farm. On the site of the present churchyard was a temple and Christian church built in the fourth century. The Baths, Basilica and Forum were all first century.

Nearby, just outside the north-east corner of the wall, are the remains of the elliptical Roman Ampitheatre which could hold the entire population. The arena measures 180 feet by 120 feet, slightly smaller than the one at Caerleon, but like it its banks were revetted with flint and tiles and supported tiers of wooden seats.

Having formed an army, King Arthur marched on York against the Saxons and defeated Colgrin and his army, which included Picts and Scots, on the River Douglas. He besieged Colgrin at York, but then returned to London to seek military aid from Hoel, the King of Brittany (then called Armorica), who landed at Southampton. With Hoel's help Arthur had a succession of victories against the Saxons, Picts and Scots at Lincoln, Caledon wood and at Bath. He also defeated his enemy in two engagements at Moray and Loch Lomond, and thereafter took York.

After restoring Loth, Urian and Auguselus to their lands, he married Guinevere, one of the fairest ladies in the land of noble Roman birth. Geoffrey of Monmouth claimed then, that Arthur defeated King Gilmaurius of Ireland before overcoming Iceland, Gotland and the Orkneys.

ARTHUR'S COURT AT CAERLEON

At Caerleon beside the River Usk in South Wales, he summoned the leaders of all the nations that he had conquered to a plenary court where the Roman legates of Lucius Hiberius arrived in truculent mood to demand tributes from Arthur for the tyrannical way his armies had overrun and subdued nations of their empire. But disregarding their haughty claims, Arthur replied contemptuously that if any tributes were due, the Romans were above all in his debt.

According to Geoffrey, the city of Caerleon was founded by Belius on the River Usk and capital of Demetia (Wales). It was chosen by Arthur as the venue of the Whitsun Plenary Court for all Europe. It then had two churches, dedicated to martyr Julius and to the blessed Aaron, the champion of Julius. It had a monastery of canons and was rated as the third most important see in Britain. Astronomy and other Arts were taught at a college by 200 learned men, and it was the duty and responsibility of astronomists to predict Arthur's future.

At the Whitsun gathering, a great many noble men and kings from at home and abroad, assembled at Caerleon, and at the feast archbishops were led to the palace in order to place the crown upon Arthur's head. Dubricius, the Archbishop of Caerleon, led the singing of mass at the crowning, and afterwards he conducted the enrobed king with due pomp to the church of the metropolitan see. There were two archbishops, one to his right and another to his left, and preceding him were the kings of Albany, Cornwall, Demetia and Venedotia, each with a golden sword, and accompanying them were clerics of every rank chanting in exquisite harmony.

Lavishly attired and attended, the queen, Guinevere, was escorted to the Church of the Virgins, with the four consorts of the King preceding her with choirs and sweet music, each carrying a white dove. Also attending were Kay the Seneschal, and 1000 noblemen, all in ermine, who bore in the food. The equivalent number of noblemen attired in miniver, followed Sir Bedivere the Cup-bearer, and assisted him with the wine. Similar duties were performed in the queen's palace where the women feasted separately, scorning to give their love to any Knight who had not proved himself three times in battle. 'In this way the womenfolk became more chaste,' wrote Geoffrey, 'and more virtuous, and for their love the Knights were even more daring.'

After the feast the two groups adjourned separately to the meadows to watch the jousting play in imitation battle, in which one knight tilted at another in tourney, while the women watched from high on the city walls. Their flirtatious behaviour frequently provoked the knights to great feats of daring and endeavour to win the lady of their choice. They competed with bows and arrows, hurled lances, tossed heavy stones and rocks, and gambled with dice. King Arthur was extremely generous with rewards and prizes on the fourth day. Many were awarded with grants of cities, castles, archbishoprics and other landed possessions. But the occasion ended on somewhat of a sour note when Roman envoys, bearing olive branches, admonished Arthur for his European adventures.

Caerleon itself was built by the early Roman invaders and became the

The Great Hall and Round Table, Winchester Castle,
Malory's. Camelot. (Winchester City Council).

17

St. Michael's Mount, near Penzance, Cornwall, said to be part of the Mythical Lyonesse

Tintagel Castle and Merlins Cave

Gateway to Tintagel Castle

Ruins of Monastery on the Tintagel Headland

Battlements of Tintagel Castle, Cornwall

Castle Bay, Tintagel

23

Tintagel Post Office, 14th Century

Dunster Castle, Somerset, where, it is said, Arthur lived as a youth

Silchester, Hampshire, where Arthur was crowned King

Roman Amphitheatre, Carleon, Ancient city's wall and trench in background

27

Carisbrook Castle, Isle of Wight

wintering quarters of the Imperial Legions. Remnants of their barracks and the city's defences may still be seen. It appears from what Geoffrey writes that Arthur made it one of his main camps. Nowhere does he mention Camelot which was a later development in the Arthurian legend and is now associated with South Cadbury in Somerset. But some historians believed that Caerleon was Camelot and that the Round Table was situated in the centre of the Roman Amphitheatre there.

Oval in shape the interior measures 184 feet long by 136½ feet wide. Other than being the place of plenary meetings, it was in Roman times the venue of gladiatorial bouts, games, animal baiting and military displays. The spectators sat on wooden seats arranged in tiers against the revetted sloping walls, which at their highest point then were 28 feet and suitably bedecked with awnings, drapes, bunting and flags.

THE MARCH AGAINST ROME

In Geoffrey's version of the life of Arthur, the legendary King's next adventure was against the imperial legions of Rome. With an army of 183,300 he set out for the Continent and on the way killed at Mont St. Michel a giant who had been terrorising the neighbourhood, and then proceeded to advance on the Roman legions which he defeated at Autun.

Arthur had left his wife Guinevere, and his nephew Mordred to govern Britain in his absence. But when Arthur reached the Alps on the way to Rome, he learnt of Mordred's treachery, for he had seized Guinevere and the Kingdom, claiming that Arthur was dead and that the throne, therefore, was rightfully his. Hearing of this Arthur immediately returned to Britain with his army.

Expecting this move, Mordred had earlier enlisted the aid of Saxon mercenaries to help him defeat Arthur when he landed at Richborough. It was a hard fight in which Gawain was killed, but Mordred was put to flight. The armies met again at Winchester, where once more Mordred fled the field of battle toward Cornwall. Arthur followed in hot pursuit. It is said that they met for the last time at Slaughter Bridge over the River Camel at Camelford in Cornwall.

THE LAST FIGHT

King Arthur had 6666 men in a division; Mordred a squadron. Those who died under Mordred's leadership were Chelric, Elaf, Egbrict and Bruning, all of them Saxons; the Irishmen Gillapatric, Gillasel and Gillarvus; and the Scots and Picts, with nearly everyone in command of them.

On Arthur's side the dead included Odbrict, King of Norway; Aschil, King of Denmark; Cador Limenich and Cassivelaunus, with many thousands of the King's soldiers, some of them Britons, others from various nations whom he had brought with him. 'Arthur, himself, our renowned King,' wrote Geoffrey, 'was mortally wounded and was carried off to the Isle of Avalon, so that his wounds might be attended to. He handed the crown of Britain over to his cousin Constantine, the son of Cador, Duke of Cornwall: This in the year 542 after our Lord's Incarnation.'

SOUTHAMPTON

Hampshire and the Isle of Wight have many Arthurian associations in Silchester, Winchester, Southampton, Portsmouth, Freshwater and Bonchurch. Southampton is where King Hoel I of Brittany, Arthur's first cousin, met the British monarch with a large army which he led to assist him in his fight àgainst the Saxons at York. Southampton was mentioned again by Geoffrey as being the port from which Arthur, with an army of 183,000 men, sailed to Barfleur, intending to defeat the Romans. He took with him some men from the Isle of Wight and other British islands.

PORTSMOUTH

At Portsmouth, it is claimed, King Arthur's army was overwhelmed in AD 501 (Anglo-Saxon Chronicle) in an indecisive battle against the invading Saxons under the leadership of Port and his two sons Bieda and Maegla. According to Laud, they came with two ships to Britain at a place called Portsmua (Portsmouth Ha) where they seized land, 'and slew a young Briton, a very noble man'.

Some scholars contend that the 'very noble man' was Geraint, one of Arthur's bravest Knights and a prince of Devon. There is a 13th-century Celtic poem which describes the battle of Llongborth (Portsmouth). Here are a few relevant lines:

At Llongborth I saw Arthur,
Brave soldiers from Devon's lowlands,
And before they were crushed, they had killed......

When Geraint was born, heaven's gates were open.
Christ gave what was asked,
A noble form, glory of Britain.

In the *Idylls of the King* by Alfred Tennyson, Geraint and Enid end their days happily until Geraint is slain in battle when fighting the Saxons:

......He crowned
A happy life with a fair death, and fell
in battle, fighting for the blameless King.

Geraint appears in *The Gododdin* of Aneirin, a sixth-century poem describing the battle of Catterick (Catraeth), fought between the British and the northern Angles in AD 598. The Geraint in this case was a descendant of the former, possessing all his qualities:

'Geraint from the South gave the war-cry,
Bright and fair, fair-formed was his face,
Generous, spear-lord, praiseworthy lord,
So gracious, well I knew his nature,
Well I knew Geraint: kind, noble, he was.'

Another Geraint, king of the British, fought Ine, king of the Saxons, in 710. Ine tried unsuccessfully to conquer Dumnonia (Devon and Cornwall) but was defeated during an invasion of Cornwall in 722.

The Roman equivalent of Geraint was *Gerontius,* and the village of Gerrans in Cornwall is derived from that name.

There is a legend that when Geraint of Llongborth fame died he was buried in Veryan Beacon, after his body had been rowed across Gerrans Bay in a golden boat with silver oars. He is said to have been the father of Cadwy, the prince with whom Arthur spent his youth at Dunster.

The battle of Llongborth (Portsmouth) was undoubtedly fought in the vicinity of the moated Porchester castle which was built by the Romans. It lies on the north shore of the harbour, and was easily accessible for shallow-draught fighting vessels. The Roman walls are remarkably well preserved, so too are the Landgate and Watergate. Early Saxon remains, of a long house and pottery were discovered within the walls of the fort, and we know that Britons occupied the castle and defended it when the Saxons, in 501, attacked it under their leader Port.

WINCHESTER - THE ROUND TABLE LEGEND

In the Great Hall of Winchester Castle is displayed 'King Arthur's Round Table' made in the reign of Edward III. Obviously then the Table never existed in the time of Arthur for the legend surrounding it was the figment of a Norman's imagination centuries later. The Table originally had legs and was first painted, probably, in 1522 on the orders of Henry VIII for the first visit of Charles V.

It has 24 segments alternating in colour between green and white with the red rose of the Tudors at its centre. In one broad segment there is a portrait

31

of King Arthur - which is fact depicts King Henry VIII - seated in the full regalia of a monarch, and in the surrounding segments are inscribed the names of his 24 Knights with Sir Galahad on his left-hand side at the place marked 'Siege Perilous.'

In some versions of the legend the Round Table was originally made by Merlin for Uther Pendragon, Arthur's father, and when he died Merlin gave it to Arthur and his Knights - the idea being that none should feel more privileged than another, and that it symbolised the roundness of the world and the zodiac. Wace the Norman, invented the story of the Round Table in *Li Romans de Brut* (1155):

> 'This Round Table was ordained that when his fair fellowship sat to meat their chairs should be high alike, their service equal, and none before or after his comrade. Thus no man could boast that he was exalted above his fellow......'

The Great Hall of Malory's Camelot dates from 1232-40 and was built by Henry III. It stands near Winchester's Roman West Gate, restored as an early medieval structure. In the Dark Ages (c. 500) urban life in Winchester was virtually non-existent and the only buildings of any note were the Palace and Minster, on a site now occupied by the cathedral, but there were villages in the neighbourhood of the Roman city walls with accompanying cemeteries.

CAMELOT - WINCHESTER OR CADBURY?

Camelot was never mentioned in the original account of Arthur's life written by Geoffrey of Monmouth, and though Malory identifies it as Winchester, William Caxton referred in his Preface to the 'toune of Camelot which dyvers now lyvying hath seen' in Wales, meaning either Caerwent or Caerleon in South Wales. But a strong superstition among the inhabitants of South Cadbury in Somerset, on the A303 between Wincanton and Ilchester, maintains that Cadbury Castle was Camelot. Nearby are a village named Queen Camel and the river Cam. Archaeological digs in the sixties produced some evidence here to confirm the existence of a fifth and sixth-century community and fortifications. Leland found traditions there, and Drayton in the *Polyolbion,* refers to it as being by the river Ivel in Somerset:

> The nearest neighbouring place to Arthur's ancient seat,
> Which made the Britons' name through all the world so great.
> Like Camelot what place was ever yet renowned?

Selden, the illustrator of Drayton's poem, writes: 'By South Cadbury is that Camelot a hill of a mile compass at the top, four trenches circling it, and twixt each of them an earthen wall'. Actually, the area between the castle ramparts on the hilltop is eighteen acres.

32

FROM MALORY TO TENNYSON

Sir Thomas Malory's *Le Morte d'Arthur* was published by William Caxton on 31 July 1485. The Caxton edition, with all its impressions and reprints, was the only text in existence until another was discovered in 1934. The more authentic text was found by W.F. Oakeshott in a 15th-century manuscript in the Fellows' Library of Winchester College, and it became possible to separate the texts (Eugéne Vinaver, in 'Sir Thomas Malory', from *Arthurian Literature in the Middle Ages,* edited by Roger Sherman Loomis), revealing the extent of Caxton's editing.

Influences on Malory

The Arthur legend had gained spiritual and romantic content, influenced more by the French, perhaps, than by the Celtic myths of Wales, Ireland and Cornwall. Conquest of these islands had opened the flood-gates to the Arthurian legends, manufactured in Europe. When Eleanor of Aquitaine came over here she brought with her minstrels and bards who soon propogated their lays and legends throughout the country.

Sir Gawain & the Green Knight

Of the numerous English verses composed then, *Sir Gawain and the Green Knight, The Marriage of Sir Gawain, Morte Arthure* and Chaucer's *The Wife of Bath's Tale,* rank as some of the best. The first, by an unknown poet, depicts the court of Camelot, into which the Green Knight advances without invitation, where he challenges Arthur to a fight. But the challenge is accepted instead by Sir Gawain, who beheads the Green Knight, representing Satan or Evil at Arthur's court. Though beheaded, the Green Knight challenges Gawain to a further duel provided he can resist several trials and temptations; one being the amorous advances of the Green Knight's wife. He succeeds in his several tasks, but cannot avoid accepting her magic girdle, the penalty for which is suffering a cut on the neck from his opponent.

Gawain nevertheless passes the test of a true knight of the Round Table. Some people claim that this poem first suggested the British award of the Order of the Garter, which is bestowed on the greatest citizens of this country. Gawain also appears as Arthur's nephew under several names in the Welsh Triads and the *Mabinogion,* where he is known as Gwalchmei. Geoffrey in his *History* spells his name Walgainus.

Much of Geoffrey's Arthur is based on the Welsh legends in the *The Mabinogion,* Celtic tales told over the centuries and eventually written down in the thirteenth. Below are derivations of names in this collection, many of which tell, perhaps for the first time, fanciful stories about Arthur and his relatives. Some of the people and objects named are: Kei - Sir Kay; Drystan - Tristram; Essyllt - Iseult (Tristram's lover); Kelliwic - the parish of Egloshayle, Wadebridge in Cornwall; Caledvwlch - Excalibur; Rhongomynyad - Arthur's cutting spear; Wynebgwrthucher - Arthur's shield; Carnwennan - Arthur's knife; Cavall - Arthur's dog. This is just a small selection, but there are many more characters and objects named allegedly associated with Arthur. Gildas Caw and Arthur's feud with his brother Hueil Caw, who lived in Strathclyde, are brothers, it is claimed, of a very large family. In the same tale, *The Dream of Rhonabwy,* Arthur is accredited with another son, Llacheu.

Arthur's battles in Caledonia and in the Lincolnshire area are believed by some scholars, to be associated with the conflicts with the Caw family. The death of Hueil, and the lifelong feuds between branches of the family, are possibly the underlying reasons why Gildas failed to mention Arthur in his chronicle, *(De Excidio Brittonum* c.548).

The family was driven south to Wales by the constant threat of Pictish raids. Hueil Caw, however, refused to move, and he and his unyielding, rebellious brothers threatened to destroy the grand alliance of British kingdoms. Arthur killed Hueil, the ring-leader, whereupon Gildas demanded compensation and Arthur generously paid. Later when Gildas moved to Glastonbury in the Somerset kingdom of Melwas (Mordred?), Arthur's wife Guinevere was kidnapped and confined at the abbey. Furious, Arthur approached Glastonbury with his levies intent on doing battle to rescue her. Gildas was sent to negotiate a treaty, and Guinevere was released. This story* is supposedly the basis of Mordred's treachery and abduction of Guinevere when Arthur was marching against Rome, as related by Geoffrey of Monmouth in *The History of the Kings of Britain.*
*Ref., *The Life of St. Gildas,*
        by Caradoc of Llancarfan.

When Sir Thomas Malory wrote *Le Morte d'Arthur,* it was as though he had grafted cuttings from every offshoot of the Arthurian legend - Breton, Norman & Celtic - on to one stem which then flourished as never before; his interpretation of the legend brilliantly conveying the romance, mysticism, chivalry and courage of the Knights of the Round Table. In it were the convoluted tales of Arthur's birth, coronation and marriage, the magic of Merlin, the tournaments, adventures, intrigues of the knights, the tragic loves of Tristram, Iseult and King Mark; of Arthur, Guinevere and Sir Lancelot; the quest for the Sangrail and how Sir Galahad is proved to be the best Knight of all; and then penultimately, treachery, betrayal and the dissolution of the Round Table. The story ends with the internecine struggle at Camlann, the death of the treacherous Sir Mordred, and Arthur, mortally wounded, is borne away magically to Avillion (Avalon). Though he dies at Glastonbury, the legend is that he will return with chivalry, gallantry and courage to defend this land against her enemies. On his tomb, says Malory, was inscribed 'Hic Iacet Arthurus, Rex Quondam Rexque Futurus' ('Here lies Arthur, the once and future king').

Edmund Spenser's Arthur

From this magnificent assemblage of the Arthurian legends, blossomed the ethereal poetry of Edmund Spenser's *The Faery Queene.* In this divine allegory, Spenser sought favours from members of the Royal Court. Prince Arthur symbolizes 'magnificence' in the Aristotelian sense, writes Spenser. His quest is to seek the Faery Queene, and he enters into the exploits of other knights. Edmund Spenser's poetry influenced Milton, Dryden, Sir Walter Scott, William Wordsworth and the entire Romantic revival of English poetry to Tennyson, Matthew Arnold, William Morris, R.S. Hawker, Algernon Swinburne and Thomas Hardy. It seems the ripples of the Arthurian legend spread endlessly over the waters of our romantic literature.

There was a strong revival of interest in the Arthurian legend in the fifteenth century, when Caxton published Malory's work. Indeed Henry VII was so convinced that the Tudors were direct descendants in the royal line from Arthur - who is said to have had two sons, Amir and Llacheu, and a daughter, Anna - that he sent a commission into Wales to trace his ancestry through the heroes of Geoffrey of Monmouth's Chronicles to the fabulous Brutus. He claimed also that the name Britain was derived from Brutus the Trojan exile who first led his people to settle these islands. This was too much for Richard III who considered Henry Tudor to be an upstart with 'no manner of right, interest, title or colour' in the kingship. But because Malory's *Le Morte d'Arthur* was issued in 1485 intense interest in the legend would not easily be dispelled. Taking advantage of this Henry VII staked his claim to the Royal Arthurian lineage by ensuring that his son was born at Winchester and was christened Arthur - Arthurus Secundus - on 19 September 1486.

Young Arthur was then created Prince of Wales and was contracted by treaty with Spain to marry Catherine, the daughter of Ferdinand King of Aragon and Isabella Queen of Castile. But before the marriage could be consummated Arthur died suddenly at Ludlow on 2 April 1502, at the age of 26 - a terrible blow to both his parents.

The greatest honour that can be bestowed upon a Briton is for

Arthurian chivalry - the Order of the Garter. Said to have been founded by Edward III, the Order originally had a membership of 26. Now, the honoured wear a ribbon of dark blue velvet below the left knee. Embroidered on it in gold is the legend *Honi soi qui mal y pense.* According to Froissart, it dates from 1344. Although the Order of the Garter had Arthurian associations to begin with, these were soon dropped. Nevertheless there were numerous Round Table meetings held on the Continent, the earliest dating from 1223. The venue was Cyprus, according to R.S. Loomis, and it was in imitation of the Knights of the Round Table, when the Lord of Beirut celebrated the knighting of his eldest sons. At Acre the Cypriot Henry II was crowned King of Jerusalem amidst such celebrations. Often there were jousts, and on some occasions there were injuries and fatalities.

Tournaments in imitation of the Round Table were attended by Kings and Queens from the thirteenth century till as late as 1493, when 2000 guests were invited to the castle at Sandricourt, near Pontoise, and stayed eight days. In England now our only symbolic link with the Arthurian legend is the ideal of the Round Table. In our history there have not been very many Kings or Princes who have measured up to Arthur's standards except Alfred The Great, and, according to Tennyson, Prince Albert, the consort of Queen Victoria.

Tennyson found the Prince to be very cordial and impressed him as being a man of strong and self-sacrificing nature. Indeed over the years a sincere respect grew and strengthened between them. The Prince admired the poet and his work, and in the Arthurian legends he came to identify himself with the good King Arthur.

The *Idylls* of 1859 were allegories representing King Arthur as 'the Ideal Soul of Man coming in contact with the warring elements of the flesh,' wrote his eldest son Hallam. These showed the different ways in which men regard Conscience, 'some reverencing it as a heaven-born King, others ascribing to it an earthly origin.' Hallam explained that his father had made the old legends his own, 'restored the idealism, and infused into them a spirit of modern thought and of ethical significance; setting his characters in a rich and varied landscape; as indeed otherwise these archaic stories would not have appealed to the world at large.'

Some critics disagreed with the concept of turning King Arthur and his Knights into Victorians with Victorian morals, but what other way was there of presenting an essentially mythical figure to a contemporary reading public. Both Malory and Spenser had done precisely the same thing with the Arthurian legend in their own lifetime by employing allegory and by addressing their works to individual patrons in the expectation of payment of money or favours.

Tennyson met Prince Albert, Queen Victoria's Consort, not long after he moved into Farringford House, Freshwater, in the Isle of Wight (1853).

From that moment onwards they became firm friends. The Royal family greatly admired their Poet Laureate's work. Most of the *Idylls of the King* were written at Farringford.

Prince Albert died in 1861, and the effect on Queen Victoria was as traumatic as Tennyson's loss of his friend Arthur Henry Hallam, and knowing what great suffering had inspired his *In Memoriam,* she turned to him now in her hour of need for comfort. Albert's death had been hastened by overwork on State affairs and managing the Osborne estate. The Queen was inconsolable, for she had always regarded him as a modern-day version of King Arthur who, in her eyes, could do no wrong - although young Prince Albert Edward, no doubt, had quite different views about his father, having experienced his Teutonic brand of discipline at first-hand.

Tennyson's words 'The Crown a lonely splendour' became very true for her till the end of her days. But the unstinting compassion and sympathy shown by Tennyson - as her Poet Laureate - in their audiences and in correspondence, created an unusual bond between poet and Queen which lasted to his death.

Besides *In Memoriam* (published in 1850), *The Idylls of the King* did more to strengthen the ties of genuine friendship between the royal family and the laureate than any other of his poems. Prince Albert in one of his last letters from Buckingham Palace (17 May 1860), which was accompanied by a copy of the *Idylls,* wrote asking the poet to autograph it, and added: 'They quite kindle the feeling with which the legends of King Arthur must have inspired the chivalry of old, whilst the graceful form in which they are presented blends those feelings with the softer tone of our present age......'

But somehow Alfred Tennyson's Victorian King can never really be equated with the *dux bellorum* of the Dark Ages, the warlike Arthur visualised by William of Malmesbury in 1125, 'a man clearly not to be dreamed of in fallacious fables, but to be proclaimed in veracious histories, as one who long sustained his tottering country, and gave the shattered minds of his fellow-citizens an edge of war.'

At Mount Badon, Arthur's greatest victory, the legendary King 'made head single-handed against nine hundred of the enemy and routed them with incredible slaughter.' He halted the pagans for forty years, for as long as it took Tennyson to write the *Idylls of the King.*

TENNYSON FOLLOWS THE GLEAM

Tennyson first came under the spell of Merlin the ancient wizard of the Dark Ages when only a lad, and followed the Gleam of Arthurian legend for the rest of his days. For him it became a quest, a life-time's obsession, a magic spell which haunted him and his poetry irresistibly from 1830 till 1889 when he wrote *Merlin and the Gleam* three years before his death.

The poem is allegorical and quasi-autobiographical. In *stanza i* he explains how the magic of Merlin has haunted him from his earliest boyhood. *Stanza ii* shows how this resulted in the early Arthurian lyrics of the 1830s. The third indicates how, as the result of unsympathetic criticism, his inspiration and faith - the Gleam, that is - temporarily deserted him.

Stanza iv shows how he was inspired by romantic fancy and nature - the early imagination - resulting in the pastorals, the eclogues and English idylls. And then he seems to revert to the subject of the death of his dear friend Arthur Henry Hallam in 1834 and the resulting despair and disinclination to continue working. But in the next his faith is slowly restored, till at last he faces death with fortitude and courage, though with increased awe in 'the mystery of the Infinite.' The restoration of his faith is confirmed in the famous poem *Crossing the Bar,* written in the same year after his recovery from a serious illness.

TENNYSON'S ARTHURIAN LYRICS

Alfred Tennyson was born in 1809 and was introduced to Malory's *Le Morte d'Arthur* at an early age. *Sir Lancelot and Queen Guinevere* was partly completed in 1830, and this was followed by *The Lady of Shalott* (1832) which was based on *Donna di Scalotta,* and in no way resembled Malory's Maid of Astolat (see *Le Morte d'Arthur,* book 18 chapters 9-20), in which the Maid in healing Lancelot of his wounds, falls desperately in love with him; but he can love no other woman than Queen Guinevere, King Arthur's wife. It is partly this betrayal which destroys the Round Table dynasty and brings about the death of Arthur.

However, the original *Lady of Shalott,* being romantic and symbolical, has a simple plot in which, as Tennyson put it, 'the new-born love for something in the wide world from which she has been for so long secluded, takes her out of the region of shadows into that of realities,' and in so doing she dies for the love of Sir Lancelot. In the *Idylls* she becomes Elaine.

Sir Galahad and *Morte d'Arthur* were published in 1835, the latter, in 1842, with a prefatory poem, entitled *The Epic.* These consisted of the pre-Idyll Arthurian poems of Tennyson, and owing to severe criticism he published little until the two 1842 volumes appeared, in which the above poems were included.

However Tennyson had a staunch ally and lifelong friend in Edward Fitzgerald who contrary to popular opinion maintained that the poet's early Arthurian poetry was far superior to the later allegorical *Idylls.* They had about them, he said, that 'champagne quality' which stems from inspiration, that much abused word.

WINDERMERE, CUMBRIA

Tennyson met Edward Fitzgerald of *Omar Khayyam* fame in Cumbria and soon they were on very friendly terms, remaining so for the rest of their lives. Fitzgerald recalled that they both went for a row on Lake Windermere: 'Resting on our oars one calm day on Windermere...... and looking into the lake quite unruffled and clear, Alfred quoted from the lines he had lately read us from the MS of *Morte d'Arthur* about the lonely lady of the lake and Excalibur -

> Nine years she wrought it, sitting in the deeps
> Upon the hidden bases of the hills.

"Not bad that, Fitz, is it!"'

Nothing would induce Tennyson to call on Wordsworth, not only because he was shy by nature, but he respected the privacy of the poet he admired so much, who then lived at Rydal Mount, Ambleside.

The Rev. H. Montagu Butler, then Master of Trinity College, Cambridge, recalled telling Tennyson, after an examination of the sixth form at Harrow, that they had been set some fine passages from *Elaine,* where Lancelot says to Lavaine:

> ......in me there dwells
> No greatness, save it be some far off touch
> Of greatness to know well I am not great.
> *There* is the man,

pointing at King Arthur. Tennyson's reply was 'Yes, when I wrote that I was thinking of Wordsworth and myself.'

Fitzgerald commented that *The Epic,* which prefaced *Morte d'Arthur* in the 1842 volumes, was an attempt 'to anticipate or excuse the "faint Homeric echoes"...... to give a reason for telling an old-world tale.' However, Leigh Hunt wrote disparagingly of it, in common with other critics.

THE CORNISH & WELSH TOURS

Morte d'Arthur was eventually extended to become the concluding book of the *Idylls.* The poem drew extensively on Malory's book and on *Mabinogion* and the French romances. To provide continuity with the preceding book, *Guinevere,* in the Idylls, the poet added 169 lines to the beginning of *The Passing of Arthur,* and 28 to the end to provide a suitable climax.

Tennyson pondered for some while, in the 1840s, over the prospect of writing the *Idylls*, but he lacked confidence and feared a repetition of the vitriolic criticism he had received. Moreover, John Sterling, whose judgement he trusted, felt it would be foolish to undertake such an epic work at his time of life. That was in 1842; but after the publication of *The Princess* in 1847, he had recovered sufficient self-confidence to set out on a working holiday to Cornwall with the intention of adding to his knowledge of the Arthurian legend, when he made these notes in his letter - diary.

Tintagel, 5 June - Clomb over Isle, disappointed, went thro' the sea-tunnel - cavern over great blocks. Walls lined with shells, pink and puce jellies. Girls playing about the rocks as in a theatre.

6 June - Slate quarries, one great pillar left standing; ship under the cliff loading; dived into a cavern all polished with the waves like dark marble with veins of pink and white. Follow'd up little stream falling thro' the worn slate, smoked a pipe at little inn, dined, walked once more to the old castle darkening in the gloom.

Slaughter Bridge, Camelford, 7 June - ......Clear brook among alders. Sought for King Arthur's Stone, found it at last by a rock under two or three sycamores, walked seaward, came down by churchyard. Song from ship. (Slaughter Bridge, Camelford was formerly said to be the site of Arthur's last battle. However, historians have since discounted this idea, but admit to there having been an Anglo-Saxon battle fought there in the 9th century.)

8 June - Walked seaward. Large crimson clover; sea purple and green like a peacock's neck. 'By bays, the peacock's neck in hue.'

14 June - Read part of *Oedipus at Colonus.*

19 June - Finished reading *Fathom.* Set off for Polperro, ripple-mark, queer old narrow-streeted place, back at 9. Turf fires on the hills; jewel-fires in the waves from the oar, which Cornish people call 'bryming.'

Perranzabuloe 1 July - Museum. After dinner went to Perranzabuloe. Coast looked grey and grand in the fading light. Went into cave, Rembrandt - like light thro' the opening.

Land's End 6 July - Went to Land's End by Logan Rock, leaden-backed mews wailing on cliff, one with two young ones. Mist. Great yellow flare just before sunset. Funeral. Land's End and life's end

Lizard 8 July - The Lizard, rocks in sea, two southern eyes of England. Tamarisk hedge in flower. Round Pentreath beach, large crane's bill near Kynance, down to cove. Glorious grass-green monsters of waves. Into caves of Asparagus Island. Sat watching wave-rainbows.

11 July - Down to Lizard Cove. Smoked with workmen. Boat to several places. Saw the further ships under Penzance like beads threading the sunny shore.

Polpur 12 July - Bathed, ran in and out of cave. Down to Caerthillian, lovely clear water in cove. Lay on Pentreath beach, thunder of waves to west. Penaluna's *Cornwall.*

13 July - Bathed in Polpur Cove. Bewick - like look of trunk, cloak and carpet bag, lying on rock. Sailed, could not land at Kynance. Saw the long green swell heaving on the black cliff, rowed into Pigeonthugo, dismal wailing of mews. To St. Ives.

The poet made abortive starts with the Idylls when he printed poems privately in 1857, but later decided to withdraw them from publication. * He made no further attempt at publication until after he had completed *Maud,* a monodrama. Perhaps now he felt that he had sufficient mastery of dramatic blank verse to embark upon the arduous odyssey of the *Idylls.* Among the four *Idylls* of the 1859 edition, *Guinevere* was the most popular. In it is a moving passage in which Arthur forgives the Queen her unfaithfulness. It invariably brought tears to the eyes of reader and listener alike. The *Idylls* became a great favourite of the Royal family, and Victoria saw her Albert as a modern-day King Arthur - her Ideal Knight.

*Enid and Nimue: the True and the False, 1857, appearing again in 1859 as *The True and the False: Four Idylls of the King,* a trial book, followed by *Idylls of the King,* the same year. Ten thousand copies were sold in the first week.

It devolved to Alfred Tennyson, in *Idylls of the King,* to pursue Merlin and the Arthurian Gleam in Nennius, Geoffrey of Monmouth, Wace, Layamon, the Welsh *Mabinogion* and Sir Thomas Malory's *Le Morte d'Arthur.* He visited Glastonbury, Salisbury, Amesbury and the New Forest. In July and August, 1856, he toured Wales with his wife, Emily, and the two boys, Hallam and Lionel. He almost finished *Enid,* and the journey took them by way of Llangollen, Dolgelly, Barmouth and Cader Idris, where he heard the roar of waters, streams and cataracts 'and I never saw anything more awful than that grey veil of rain drawn straight over Cader Idris, pale light at the lower edge. It looked as if death were behind it, and made me shudder when I thought he was there. A message came from him by the guide that he had gone to Dolgelly.'

At Festiniog the roar of cataract and torrent inspired him to write

> For as one,
> That listens near a torrent mountain-brook,
> All thro' the crash of the near cataract hears
> The drumming thunder of the huger fall
> At distance, were the soldiers wont to hear
> His voice in battle.

They then journeyed through Llanidloes, Builth and arrived at Caerleon on 16 September, where he wrote: 'The Usk murmurs by the windows, and I sit like King Arthur in Caerleon. This is a most quiet, half-ruined village of about 1500 inhabitants with a little museum of Roman tombstones and other things.' Then on to Caerphilly, Methyr Tydvil, Raglan, Brecon, Gloucester, Salisbury and homeward. According to a writer in *The Mabinogion* ('Geraint and Enid') Arthur held court at Caerleon through seven Easters and five Christmases, and on one occasion at Whitsuntide, for it had the advantage of being so accessible from sea and land.

'The King had called together nine Kings with earls and barons,' continued the writer, 'a normal occurence at every feast. Thirteen churches were set aside for masses, one for Arthur and his rulers and guests, one for Gwenhwyvar (Guinevere) and her ladies, one for the stewards and suppliants, one for Odyar the Frank and other officers, and nine others for nine captains, especially Gwalchmei, he being the most distinguished for his fighting ability and noble bearing.'

Gerald of Wales, in his *Journey Through Wales,* written in the 12th century, describes it in detail (bk I, ch v): 'It was constructed with great care,' he writes, 'by the Romans, the walls being built of brick. You can still see many vestiges of its one-time splendour. There are immense palaces, which, with the gilded gables of their roofs, once rivalled the magnificence of ancient Rome...... Caerleon is beautifully situated on the bank of the River Usk. When the tide comes in, ships sail right up to the city. It is surrounded by woods and meadows. It was here that the Roman legates came to seek audience of the great Arthur's famous court.'

With the help of local teachers and historians, Tennyson and Emily were able to learn some Welsh, reading *Hanes Cymru* (Welsh History), *Llywarch Hen* and the *Mabinogion,* which was first translated by Lady Charlotte Guest. It is a collection of fanciful tales mostly handed down by word of mouth, and one of these tales, *Geraint and Enid,* became the basis of his own Idylls *Enid, The Marriage of Geraint* and *Geraint and Enid* (the latter two an expansion of the first). The *Mabinogion* romances 'Owein,' 'Peredur' and 'Gereint' are very similar to the French *Yvain, Perceval* and *Erec,* all having Arthurian themes.

The following lines were written on Tennyson Down behind Farringford, Freshwater, West Wight, and are taken from 'Geraint and Enid' in the *Idylls of the King:*

> He spoke, and one among his gentlewomen
> Displayed a splendid silk of foreign loom,
> Where like a shoaling sea the lovely blue
> Played into green, and thicker down the front
> With jewels than the sward with drops of dew,
> When all night long a cloud clings to the hill,
> And with the dawn ascending lets the day
> Strike where it clung: so thickly shone the gems.

Some of the *Idylls* were written out as prose first before being translated into verse. These were: *The Holy Grail, Pelleas and Ettarre, Gareth and Lynette,* and *Balin and Balan.* A passage from the latter confirms the rumour of Queen Guinevere's adulterous love for Sir Lancelot:

> And when he stood as Lot's wife stood, salt-petrified, and stared at her, she cried again, 'Sir Knight, ye need not gaze thus at me as if I were a reder of fables and a teller of false tales. Now let me tell thee how I saw myself Sir Lancelot and the Queen within a bower at Camelot but twelve months since and heard her say, "O sir, my lord Sir Lancelot, for thou indeed art my true lord, and none other save by the law."'

Tennyson had always envisaged Arthur as the ideal man after he had read the following passage from Joseph of Exeter: 'The old world knows not his peer, nor will the future show us his equal: he alone towers over other Kings, better than the past ones and greater than those that are to be.' *Brut ab Arthur* confirms this: 'In short God has not made since Adam was, the man more perfect than Arthur.'

But though Tennyson had immersed himself so profoundly in the Arthurian legend from his earliest years, he was yet afraid to embark on the frightening odyssey of writing the epic *Idylls of the King;* the *Holy Grail* in particular, because he feared lest he should incur a charge of irreverence.

After the favourable reception of the first edition of the *Idylls of the King* (1859), which included *Enid, Vivien, Elaine* and *Guinevere,* the poet set out from his Isle of Wight home to extend his research into the Arthurian legend, to be able to add to the series. He arrived at Bideford on 21 August 1860, and after a couple of days there journeyed south through Bude to Boscastle and Tintagel.

25 August. Arrived at Tintagel. Black cliffs and caves and storm and wind, but I weather it out and take my ten-miles-a-day walks in my weather-proofs. Palgrave arrived today.

28th. Tintagel. We believe that we are going tomorrow to Penzance, or in that direction. We have had two fine days and some exceedingly grand coast views. Here is an artist, a friend of Woolner's (Inchbold), sketching now in this room. I am very tired of walking against wind and rain. (H. Tennyson's *Memoir*).

Here Palgrave filled in some details about their activities:
'At a sea inlet of wonderful picturesqueness, so grandly modelled are the rocks which wall it, so translucently purple the waves that are its pavement - waves when the naked babe Arthur came ashore in flame -stand the time-eaten ruins of unknown date which bear the name Tintagel. To these of course we climbed - descending from the "castle gateway by the chasm," and at a turn in the rocks meeting that ever graceful, ill-appreciated landscapist, Inchbold: whose cry of delighted wonder at sight of Tennyson still sounds in the sole survivor's ear. Thence, after some delightful wandering walks, by a dreary road (for such is often the character of central Cornwall), we moved to Camelford on the greatly-winding stream which the name indicates. Near the little town, on the edge of the river, is shown a large block of stone upon which legend places Arthur, hiding or meditating, after his last fatal battle. It lay below the bank; and in his eagerness to reach it and sit down (as he sat in 1851 on that other, the *Sasso di Dante* by Sta. Maria del Foire), Arthur's poet slipped right into the stream, and returned laughing to Camelford.
'The next halting-place I remember was Penzance; whence by Marazion, we crossed to and saw our English smaller but yet impressive and beautiful St Michael's Mount.'

31 August. Union Hotel, Penzance...... I have now walked 10 miles a day for 10 days, equal 100, and I want to continue doing that for some time longer. I am going tomorrow to Land's End and then I must return here, and then I go to the Scilly Isles and then again return here.

5 September. Land's End Inn..... We are here at this racketry rather dirty inn, but we have had four glorious days and *magnificently coloured seas*. Today the Scilly Isles look so dark and clear on the horizon that one expects rain.

EAST VIEW of the *KINGS HOUSE* & THE *ADJOINING OFFICES*, as intended to have been finished by *SIR CHRIST.* *WREN.*

Winchester Castle

45

The Round Table, Winchester

46

S. Cadbury Castle, Somerset.S. Cadbury village is below left; Sutton Moutis, top right; and below, Little Weston. The River Cam flows from beside the Castle past the north side of Little Weston.

47

South Cadbury Castle

48

South Cadbury Castle

49

Tennyson's Isle of Wight House, Farringford, Freshwater, Isle of Wight

Swainston - The home of Tennyson's great friend, Sir John Simeon. The poet was a frequent visitor, and wrote much of his verse here.

Alfred Lord
Tennyson
(aged 80 years)

The Tennyson Memorial on
Tennyson Down, Freshwater,
Isles of Wight.

9 September. St Mary's, Scilly Isles. Captain Tregarthen who has the packet and the hotel here, has brought me my letters: the packet only goes three times a week. I shall stop here till Wednesday; there are West Indian Aloes here 30 feet high, in blossom, and out all the winter, yet the peaches wont ripen; vast hedges of splendid geraniums, a delight to the eye, yet the mulberry won't ripen. These Islands are very peculiar and in some respects very fine. I never saw anything quite like them.

Tennyson admitted frankly that the poem 'The Quest of the Sangraal' (1863) by the Rev. Robert Steven Hawker, whom he had met at Morwenstow rectory in 1848, was far superior to his own version. The rector on that occasion had supplied Tennyson with much useful folklore and mythology, and Hawker's description of a shipwreck was used in 'The Passing of Arthur:' '...... only the wan wave / Brake in among dead faces, to and fro / Swaying the helpless hands, and up and down / Tumbling the hollow helmets of the fallen,...... / And rolling far along the gloomy shores / The voice of days of old and days to be.' (129-135).

LYONESSE

Traditionally the home of Sir Galahad and Tristram, Lyonesse was a mythical land lying between Cornwall and the Isles of Scilly. Doubtless land was there 5,000 years ago, but certainly not during the Dark Ages, c.500. However there is good reason to believe that the main islands of Scilly - St. Mary's, St. Agnes, St. Martins, Tresco, Bryher and St. Helens -were one at the time of the Roman occupation of Britain, judging by the exposure of submarine walls and fields and relics of that period, 20 feet below the normal surface of the sea. The photograph of Mounts Bay at Springtide, showing the exposure of an ancient forest tends also to substantiate the concept of a sunken land. According to local inhabitants coast-fishermen have trawled masonry in their nets from the area surrounding Seven Stones. On Tresco there is a medieval ruined church containing a 5th or 6th-century tomb inscribed as follows:
'......THI FILI......COGVI'. On St. Martins in 1948 Roman pottery was discovered with pieces of 'cassiterite - tin ore,' as well as first-century Roman bronze brooches, second-century potsherds, fragments of Samian ware, a small load of coins of the reign of Constantine II, and a Roman altar at Valhalla on Tresco. In the Middle Ages St. Helen's was named St. Lide's Isle, from Elidius, who was the son of a King and Bishop. In those days St. Helen's was the resort for Christian pilgrims.

Two of these enchanted islands are named Great Arthur and Little Arthur, and may be seen to their best advantage when travelling from Penzance to St. Mary's by helicopter. On Halangy Down, St. Mary's, are the remains of a Romano-British village and Bants Carn which date from the 2nd and 3rd centuries. The view from them embraces Samson, Bryher, Tresco, St. Helen's, The Round Island and St. Martin's, which in Arthur's time were a single island, the islands themselves forming its outer rim. Hence the Tennysonian metaphor - 'The phantom circle of a moaning sea.'

Within the basin formed by the circle of islands, traces of field walls and other structures may be seen at lowtide between Samson and Tresco and St. Martin's and St. Mary's islands. At such times when tides are at their lowest ebb, it is possible to walk from Tresco, for example, to Bryher, which indicates the shallowness of sea in this central basin.

The Cornish journeys inspired Tennyson to add more, and yet more sections to the *Idylls* till ultimately, by 1885, he had completed the twelve parts of his magnum opus: 1 - *The Coming of Arthur;* 2 - *Gareth and Lynette;* 3 - *The Marriage of Geraint;* 4 - *Geraint and Enid;* 5 - *Balin and Balan;* 6 - *Merlin and Vivien;* 7 - *Lancelot and Elaine;* 8 - *The Holy Grail;* 9 - *Pelleas and Ettarre;* 10 - *The Last Tournament;* 11 - *Guinevere;* 12 - *The Passing of Arthur.*

Closest to Tennyson's heart, undoubtedly, was the later Idyll which began as *Morte d'Arthur,* and was written as a direct result of the death of his dear friend Arthur Henry Hallam in 1833. Hallam was a young man of brilliant intellect and with great scholarly expectations, with the noblest and most Christian of natures. Tennyson was devastated with grief and temporarily lost faith in the Church. His elegy to A.H. Hallam, *In Memoriam,* depicts the restoration of his Christian faith, and the agonising recovery from bereavement. It was published in 1850 and secured him the Poet laureateship. The original King Arthur of *Morte d'Arthur* was based on his dead friend's character and therefore assumes some importance in its execution. It should be considered in conjunction with *In Memoriam AHH.*

At Cambridge, Tennyson was admitted to the company of the Apostles, an élite group of intellectuals who debated and discussed politics, religion and literature. He became the intimate friend of Arthur Henry Hallam, the brilliant son of the historian Henry Hallam, and with him, in 1830, he toured the Pyrenees mountains and gave financial aid to the Spanish revolutionaries who were attempting to overthrow the King. In the same year Alfred published *Poems, Chiefly Lyrical* which was severely criticised by 'Christopher North' in *Blackwood's Magazine.*

Arthur Hallam was engaged to Alfred's sister, Emily, but during a tour in Austria in 1833, he suddenly was taken ill and died. Alfred was distraught at the news and soon started writing his elegies in memory of his friend. At the same time he wrote 'Two Voices,' 'Ulysses,' 'St. Simeon Stylites,' 'St. Agnes' Eve,' 'Lancelot and Guinevere,' 'Sir Galahad' and 'The Beggar Maid.' He had also begun work on 'Morte d'Arthur.' His *Poems 1833,* provoked a vitriolic attack by John Wilson Crocker in the *Quarterly Review.*

One particular passage in *Morte d'Arthur* reflects poignantly the poet's anguish in losing Arthur Hallam, when King Arthur, mortally wounded, says to Sir Bedivere:

> The old order changeth, yielding place to new,
> And God fulfills himself in many ways,
> Lest one good custom should corrupt the world.
> Comfort thyself: what comfort is in me?
> I have lived my life, and that which I have done
> May He within himself make pure! but thou,
> If thou should'st never see my face again,
> Pray for my soul. More things are wrought by prayer
> Than this world dreams of. Wherefore, let thy voice
> Rise like a fountain for me night and day.
> For what are men better than sheep or goats
> That nourish a blind life within the brain,
> If, knowing God, they lift not hands of prayer
> Both for themselves and those who call them friends?

In the Prologue to *In Memoriam AHH,* Tennyson addresses the 'Strong Son of God,' and reasons that, though He is spiritual and unseen, we must still have faith in His existence. He has created Life and Death and deals equally fairly with both. Life is incomprehensible for why must man die? Nevertheless if it is God's will, so be it, for He is just. Although our wills are ours, yet are we bound by the divine will of God (cp. 'Morte d'Arthur:' 'For so the whole round earth is in every way / Bound by gold chains about the feet of God.'). Our faith must be blind, but as knowledge is acquired, so faith increases. The poet seeks forgiveness for grieving over the loss of Arthur Hallam for so long, but he now believes that this friend lives in the divine God of Love. He seeks forgiveness, too, for his wild cries of grief and especially where he had deviated from the truth. He asks the God of Wisdom to make him wise.

SEASONAL MOODS

Parts of the *Idylls of the King* were written on the Isle of Wight in a little summer-house at the rear of the Farringford House copse overlooking the down, and it is known that some of the descriptive passages suggest his observation of local topography. But in the end he was so besieged with admirers and autograph-hunters that he was forced to seek refuge by building a new house, 'Aldworth.'* He had found that he could not complete *The Holy Grail* on the Island, but when he stayed to 'Aldworth,' it came naturally to him. Tennyson said that 'The Passing of Arthur,' 'signified a temporary triumph of evil, the confusion of moral order, closing in the Great Battle of the West.'

* Near the boundary of West Sussex, not far from Haslemere.

Hallam Tennyson writes in his *Memoir:* 'My father felt strongly that only under the inspiration of ideals, and with his "sword bathed in heaven," can a man combat the cynical indifference, the intellectual selfishness, the sloth of will, the utilitarian materialism of a transition age. "Poetry is truer than fact," he would say. Guided by the voice within the Ideal Soul looks out into the Infinite for the highest Ideal and finds it nowhere realized so mightily as in the Word who "wrought with human hands the creed of creeds." But for Arthur, as for everyone who believes in the Word however interpreted, arises the question "How can I in my life, in my small measure, and in my limited sphere reflect this highest ideal?" From the answers to this question come the strength of life, its beauty, and above all its helpfulness to the world.

'To sum up: if Epic unity is looked for in the *Idylls* we find it not in the wrath of an Achilles, nor in the wanderings of a Ulysses, but in the unending war of humanity in all ages, - the world-wide war of Sense and Soul, typified in individuals, with the subtle interaction of character upon character, the central dominant figure being the pure, generous, tender, brave, human-hearted Arthur, - so that the links (with here and there symbolic accessories) which bind the *Idylls* into an artistic whole, are perhaps somewhat intricate.

'My father would explain that the great resolve (to ennoble and spiritualize mankind) is kept so long as all work in obedience to the highest and holiest law within them: in those days when all the court is one Utopia:

> The King will follow Christ, and we the King,
> In whom High God has breathed a secret thing.

Repentance: 'So in Guinevere's repentance and the King's forgiveness: so too of the repentance of Lancelot, whose innocent worship of beauty had turned into the "guilty love," and of whom we are told that he died a "holy man." But repentance could not avert the doom of the Round Table. The "last dim wierd battle" my father would quote as some of his best work and would allow that it was a "presentiment of human death" as well as of the overthrow of the "old order:"

> And even on Arthur fell
> Confusion, since he saw not what he fought.
> For friend and foe were shadows in the mist,
> And friend slew friend not knowing whom he slew,......
> And rolling far along the gloomy shores
> The voice of days of old and days to be. (98-135)

'And he liked to read the last passage in *The Passing of Arthur,* that one when Arthur himself finds the comfort of the faith with which he comforted Bedivere in his passing "from the great deep to the great deep" - for the individual may seem to fail in his purpose, but his work cannot die -

> The old order changeth, yielding place to new,
> And God fulfills himself in many ways;

and that other, when Bedivere hears from dawn, the East, whence have sprung all the great religions, the triumph of welcome given to him who proved himself "more than conqueror:"

> As from beyond the limit of the world,
> Like the last echo born of a great cry,
> Sounds, as if some fair city were one voice
> Around a King returning from his wars (458-61).

'My father made this further manuscript note on another phase of the unity of the poem. "The Coming of Arthur is on the night of the New Year; when he is wedded *the world is white with May;* on a summer night the vision of the Holy Grail appears; and thee Last Tournament, is in the *yellowing autumntide.* Guinevere flees through the mists of autumn, and Arthur's death takes place at midnight in mid-winter. The form of the "Coming of Arthur" and of the "Passing" is purposely more archaic than that of the other *Idylls.*"'

Tennyson's deep love of Nature is expressed vividly in metaphors and similes. There is a glorious richness of illustration in the beautiful diction, music and rhythm. The simplicity and lucidity of the word-ornaments enhance the grandeur of the Idylls.

OUTLINE OF THE 'IDYLLS OF THE KING'

The Coming of Arthur - Britain is in the Dark Ages. Arthur is born to Uther Pendragon and Ygerne, the Duke of Gorlois's widow. After his coronation, Arthur marries Guinevere, daughter of King Leodogran of Cameliard. Initially Arthur is not accepted as King by all the barons, but once the mystery of his parentage is resolved, most of the Knights are satisfied. Moreover he proves to be a worthy King by his generosity, courage and prowess of arms in battle. He plans to weld the petty Kingdoms and Princedoms of Britain into a grand alliance. The malignant Sir Mordred is one of the few who always doubts his royal lineage. As Arthur's nephew, his plan is to destroy the Order of the Knights of the Round Table, and usurp him.

Gareth and Lynette - Gareth the son of Lot, King of Orkney, seeks admission to the court of King Arthur against his mother's wishes. He serves Sir Kay the Seneschal for a trial period as a disguised kitchen knave. Then with his identity disclosed, he asks King Arthur's permission to replace Sir Lancelot in an adventure to rescue Lynette's sister, Lyonors, whom a Knight had abducted to his castle. Lynette despises the amorous advances of a mere kitchen knave, till won over by his prowess in defeating three of four knights in combat. The fourth is a boy disguised horribly as Death, whom he also vanquishes -

> 'And he that told the tale in olden times
> Says that Sir Gareth wedded Lyonors,
> But, he, that told it later, says Lynette.'

The Marriage of Geraint and *Geraint and Enid* - Sickened by rumours of Queen Guinevere's infidelity to Arthur in her love for Lancelot, Geraint is determined that his wife, Enid, shall be protected from the corruption of Court life. Thus, with Arthur's permission he, Enid, and a number of Knights depart, crossing the Severn to their own land in Devon. Geraint begins to imagine that Enid is unfaithful to him, and never leaves her side. No more does he hunt, nor tilt at tournaments, and becomes forgetful of his glory and his name, of his Princedom and its cares. Behind his back his people ridicule his unmanliness. But eventually he is convinced of his wife's fidelity and love for him, and Geraint and Enid spend the rest of their days happily until Geraint is slain in battle against the Saxons -

> 'When Geraint was born, heaven's gates were open:
> Christ gave what was asked,
> A noble form, glory of Britain.'

> (from the 13th-century Welsh poem
> *Elegy of Geraint*, by Llywarch Hen)

Balin and Balan - Devoted as he is to Queen Guinevere, Balin becomes so disturbed by her affair with Lancelot that he leaves Arthur's court. The perfidious Vivien confirms his suspicions, and driven to madness and despair he defaces the arms and the image of the Queen on his shield. Balan, his brother, encounters in the forest the temporarily deranged Balin who is possessed of the devil. Balan, bound on a quest for the Wood-devil, believes he has found him and the two men fight, mortally wounding each other, much to their mutual grief, when the truth is known.

Merlin and Vivien - Merlin the Mage is besotted with love for Vivien, the malignant Lady of the Lake, and in his desperate desire to be with her and make love to her, he is eventually ensnared by her wiles, when she cunningly weedles from him the secrets of his necromancy. These she uses against him when the opportunity presents itself. Merlin, 'overtalked and overworn, yielded to her, told her all the charm and slept.

'Then, in one moment, she put forth the charm
Of woven paces and of waving hands,
And in the hollow oak he lay as dead,
And lost to life and use and name and fame,

'Then crying "I have made his glory mine,"
And shrieking out "O Fool!" the harlot leapt
Adown the forest, and the thicket closed
Behind her, and the forest echoed "fool."'

Lancelot and Elaine - Arthur holds a tournament at Camelot for a prize of the last and the greatest of eight diamonds found in a crown. Because Queen Guinevere is sick, Lancelot tells Arthur he cannot attend the tourney and the King's suspicions are aroused. Guinevere entreats him to attend, but instead he travels to Astolat feeling unwilling to deceive Arthur by attending on her behalf. At Astolat he is greeted by Sir Torre, Lavaine, Elaine, the sons and daughter of the Lord of the castle, to whom he explains that though he wishes to go to the tournament, he prefers to do so incognito. Leaving his shield with Elaine, who falls in love with him, he borrows Torre's. At Elaine's request he wears on his helmet her red sleeve embroidered with pearls. Still unaware of whom he is, Lavaine accompanies him to the lists, where after sustaining a terrible wound from a spear, he defeats all-comers from the court of King Arthur. Though disguised and with an unknown crest on his shield, Arthur recognises his style of fighting, but before he can be offered the prize diamond, he disappears with Lavaine to a hermit who heals his wound. Lavaine is now aware of Lancelot's identity. Meanwhile Gawain is sent by Arthur with the prize diamond to Astolat, where he hears of Lancelot's wound and is shown his personal shield. Learning of Elaine's love for Lancelot, Gawain discloses that he loves another. Soon Elaine's love for Lancelot is noised abroad, causing great consternation at King Arthur's court. Elaine goes to Lancelot to help heal his wound. She confesses her love which is not reciprocated. When cured, he, Elaine and Lavaine return to Astolat where he collects his shield, informing her as gently as he can that he cannot love her. She is heart-broken, and as Lancelot leaves, she tells her father and brothers that she cannot live without him. Having written a final note to be taken by Lavaine to court she requests that her body be taken in a boat to Camelot, where there is much heart searching because of her death from unrequited love for Lancelot, Guinevere's paramour.

The Holy Grail - Sir Percivale takes Holy Orders at a monastery, where he tells another monk of the quest of the Holy Grail, and how Galahad proves to be purest of all the Knights of the Round Table, because he is permitted to see and receive the Holy Grail, whereas no other Knight is so privileged. Percivale merely glimpses the Grail, but cannot approach it. Honest Bors sees it, but

Gawain is disappointed. So too is Sir Lancelot, who wrestles with his soul, but cannot rid himself of the guilty love for Guinevere, which bars his way.

Pelleas and Ettarre - Pelleas, a strong youth, arrives at Arthur's court at Caerleon, asking to be made a Knight and to take part in the Tournament of Youth. He seeks to win a Knightly sword, and, for his beloved lady, Ettarre, a golden circlet. He has promised to make her as famous as Guinevere, and he as Arthur. Ettarre, a heartless vain creature, plays Pelleas along in the expectation of love, believing he may win her the golden circlet. She intends to drop him afterwards. Arthur has come to love him and excludes his older and more experienced Knights from the lists so that Pelleas, by his knightly prowess, may win his maid. He wins both sword and circlet. There Ettarre's gratitude stops - a fact remarked by Guinevere. Pelleas follows home Ettarre's entourage of Knights and servants keeping at a distance. He is excluded from her castle, and three Knights are sent to drive him away. He defeats them on all occasions. Gawain happens by and offers to go into the castle in his armour, and in doing so further his suit. Pelleas is suspicious and follows to discover Gawain's perfidy. Percivale tells Pelleas that, not only is Ettarre unfaithful, but also Guinevere, Lancelot and other Knights at Arthur's court. Pelleas vows to cleanse the Arthurian 'stables,' but is defeated by Lancelot who spares his life. Returning to Arthur's hall, all feel great sorrow that the Round Table should come to this, for it is the beginning of the end.

The Last Tournament - Tristram comes to the Tournament of the Dead Innocence. The scene is set on a wet and wintry day. The prize is a necklace of rubies once worn by a child adopted by Guinevere, but now dead. The sight of it now brings the Queen great pain. Tristram has deserted his wife, Iseult, in Brittany, and having won the tournament, he takes the prize rubies to his paramour, Queen Iseult of Tintagel, the wife of King Mark. While Tristram hangs them about her neck, King Mark rises up behind him and cleaves him though the skull. Total gloom descends upon Arthur's court. Guinevere has fled, and most of the Knights of the Round Table disbanded

> That night came Arthur home, and while he climbed......
> The stair to the hall, and looked and saw
> The great Queen's bower was dark, - about his feet
> A voice clung sobbing till he questioned it,
> 'Who art thou?' and the voice about his feet
> Sent up an answer, sobbing, 'I am thy fool
> And I shall never make thee smile again.'

Guinevere - Lancelot and Guinevere talk secretly about their future. He wishes to take her to his castle abroad, but she would rather retreat to a nunnery at Almesbury. Sir Mordred overhears them talking, but is caught by Lancelot and is thrown from his hiding place. Mordred loathes Lancelot and will only be content when he destroys the court of King Arthur. What he hears on this occasion gives him more ammunition to achieve his ambitions, to usurp Arthur on the throne of Britain and take Guinevere for his wife. But the Queen shrinks from his odious company at court. Lancelot goes away to fight Arthur, who has turned against him. In their absence Mordred recruits Saxon mercenaries to his cause to fight and kill Arthur. Meanwhile Guinevere retires to her nunnery, where, having concluded his battle against Lancelot, Arthur calls on her, rebuking her for her shameless infidelity in loving Lancelot.

Perhaps more than anyone else she is responsible for the dissolution of the Round Table. She repents, and Arthur forgives her, but he can no longer touch or live with her. So saying, he departs from her to fight his last battle against the pagan forces of Sir Mordred. As he leaves he appears to her as an angel. She lives for another three years.

The Passing of Arthur - After the battle of Camlann, Sir Bedivere, the only surviving Knight of the Round Table, describes the closing chapter of Arthur's life; how he is forewarned of his impending doom by the ghost of Gawain; how with his army he pushes the forces of Sir Mordred down the peninsula of Cornwall the western bound of Lyonesse; how in the swirling mists of the battle-field none can tell whether he fights friend or foe, till finally all lie dead or dying except Sir Mordred, their arch-enemy, and Sir Bedivere and his King, Arthur. They see Mordred standing alone among the piles of corpses, and the King challenges him, both dealing mortal blows. Mordred dies, but the King's death is lingering. He asks Bedivere to take him to a chapel to pray, and then to carry his magical sword, Excalibur, to the mere, and throw it into the centre, where it will be caught by the Lady of the Lake. Twice Bedivere lies about having thrown it, but Arthur, perceiving the truth, tells him to go again and dispose of it as he instructed. This having been done they await a boat, in which are three Queens, to take him to Avilion,

'Where falls not hail, or rain, or any snow,
Nor ever wind blows loudly; but it lies
Deep-meadowed, happy, fair with orchard lawns
And bowery hollow crowned with summer sea,
Where I will heal me of my grievous wound.'

Left alone at last, Sir Bedivere, perceiving the dawn of a New Year, exclaims:

'He passes to be King among the dead,
And after healing of his grievous wound
He comes again; but - if he come no more -
O me, be yon dark Queens in yon black boat,
Who shrieked and wailed, the three whereat we gazed

61

On that high day, when, clothed with living light,
They stood before his throne in silence, friends
Of Arthur, who should help him at his need?'

SWORD EXCALIBUR

The earliest references to Arthur's sword are in the *Mabinogion* (Celtic myths) and in Geoffrey of Monmouth's *History*. In the first it was known as 'Caledvwlch,' and the latter as 'Caliburn.' But the French first called it *Excalibur* (cut steel) in 'Walter Map's'* *The Death of King Arthur*. After him, Sir Thomas Malory and Alfred Tennyson wrote of it as Excalibur, giving it spiritual and symbolic qualities. For Tennyson it becomes a symbol of the Cross and the invincibility of moral force. Arthur accepted it from the Lady of the Lake on condition that when his life neared its end he should return it to her. The first writer entrusts this job to Sir Girflet, the faithful Knight. 'Go up that hill,' the King instructs Girflet, 'where you will find a lake, and throw my sword into it, because I do not want it to remain in this Kingdom, in case our wicked successors gain possession of it.' Malory writes: 'Therefore,' said Arthur unto Sir Bedivere, 'take thou Excalibur, my good sword, and go with it to yonder water side, and when thou comest there I charge thee throw my sword in that water, and come again and tell what thou seest.' The Tennyson version is almost indentical, but transformed into verse.

Tennyson concluded his poem where Bedivere watches Arthur disappearing from view in a barque with the three Queens, but Malory goes a stage further. Bedivere, alone in an alien world after Arthur's departure, then made his way hurriedly to Avalon where the one time Bishop of Canterbury, now a hermit, informs him that the three Queens brought Arthur's body to Glastonbury -

Yet some men say in many parts of England that King Arthur is not dead, but had by the will of Our Lord Jesu into another place; and men say that he shall come again, and he shall win the Holy Cross. I will not say that it shall be so, but rather I will say, here in this world he changed his life. But many men say that there is written upon a tomb this verse: HIC IACET ARTHURUS, REX QUONDAM REXQUE FUTURUS ('Here lies Arthur, the Once and Future King.')

Tennyson was asked if the three Queens who attended Arthur on his journey to Avalon (Avillion) were Faith, Hope and Charity; to which he replied: 'They are right, and they are not right. They mean that and they do

---

*Map's claim to the authorship is now disproved. The actual author was a Frenchman from Champagne (c.1230-35).

not. They are three of the noblest of women. They are also those three Graces, but they are much more. I hate to be tied down to say, *"This* means *that,"* because the thought within the image is much more than any one interpretation.'

In the three French-based accounts of Arthur's death, he is borne away magically to Avalon (Avillion) by three 'dark Queens,' whom Tennyson does not name, but Malory indentifies as Arthur's sister, Queen Morgan le Fay, the Queen of Northgales and the Queen of the Waste Lands. He includes another female, Nimue, the chief Lady of the Lake who had wedded the good knight Pelleas. Morgan tends Arthur's wounds on the Isle of Avalon. In a Latin poem in a Cotton MS., Arthur is piloted by Barinthus 'skilled in the navigation of the seas and in the knowledge of all the stars of heaven, hither we brought Arthur sore wounded at the battle of Camlann. With him, as captain of our barque, hither came with our Prince and Morgain received us with due honours, laid the King upon her couch covered with embroidered gold. With her own hand she uncovered the wound and examined it long. At length she declared that health might return if his stay with her be prolonged; and if he were willing to submit to her healing art.'

Although he died, a myth persists - even to this day - that Arthur will return after a long sleep. Geoffrey of Monmouth, in his book *Historia Regum Britanniae* is largely responsible for perpetuating most of the myths and legends of Arthur.

King Arthur is seen in English literature as a symbol of the incorruptible destroyed by a corrupt society. The prophet and enchanted Merlin had long ago foretold that King Arthur would become a great monarch, and would return after death, symbolizing resurrection - 'Perish by this people which I made - / Tho' Merlin sware that I should come again / To rule once more......' This superstition prevails even today among some of the old country folk - that Arthur will return to right all wrongs and polish our tarnished national image.

ARTHUR' LAST FIGHT AT CAMLANN, CAMELFORD

If the claim is true that the battle of Camlann was fought beside the River Camel, near Camelford in Cornwall, how can it be substantiated? Simply, it cannot. But historians used to believe that an inscribed stone beside the river and not far from Slaughter Bridge, was where Arthur lay after he was mortally wounded during the battle. On this stone, there is a Latin inscription partly obliterated. It reads: 'LATIN......HIC IACIT FILIVS M......AR......' which in the original could either have been 'LATINI HIC IACIT FILIVS MAGARI' or 'LATINUS HIC IACIT FILIVS MERLINI ARTURUS.' The correct version is open entirely to conjecture, but there seems to be a general concensus of opinion among historians that the former is the correct rendering, and that the inscription commemorated the death of someone in the 9th century.

THE HOLY GRAIL

......From our old books I know
That Joseph came of old to Glastonbury,
And there the heathen Prince Arviragus,
Gave him an isle of Marsh whereon to build;
And there he built with wattles from the marsh
A little lonely church in days of yore......
(Tennyson - 'The Holy Grail')

The Grail in medieval legends symbolised the vessel used by Christ at the Last Supper, in which Joseph of Aremathea received the Saviour's blood at the Cross. Only one Knight of the Round Table was perfect enough to receive the Grail, and upon his return to Camelot, Galahad occupied the seat on the left of Arthur reserved for such a person. It was called 'Siege Perilous,' which indeed the Quest had been for all the other Knights who had sought it unsuccessfully. The Quest motivated by glory-seeking, marked the beginning of the end for the Fellowship of the Round Table.

GLASTONBURY - AVALON, ARTHUR'S RESTING PLACE

Gerald of Wales witnessed the exhumation of the bones of Arthur and his second wife Guinevere in the year 1190, and he gave an account of the event in *De principis instructione,* I, 20. According to monastery records Arthur had been a munificent patron of the abbey of Glastonbury giving many donations to the monks and always supporting them strongly. Apparently he had been particularly fond of the church of the Blessed Mary, Mother of God in Glastonbury and had fostered its interests with much greater loving care than those of any of the others.

He used to go into battle with a full-length portrait of the Blessed Virgin painted on the front of his shield, so that in the heat of battle, said Gerald, 'he could gaze upon Her; and whenever he was about to make contact with the enemy, he would kiss Her feet with great devoutness.'

The tomb, a hollowed-out oak-bole, was found at a depth of more than 16 feet between two pyramids, as originally indicated. There was a stone slab with a leaden cross attached to the underside. Gerald, who saw the cross himself, had traced the lettering cut into it on the side nearest the stone. The inscription was: 'HERE IN THE ISLE OF AVALON LIES BURIED THE RENOWNED KING ARTHUR, WITH GUINEVERE, HIS SECOND WIFE.' For the first time it came to the notice of everybody present that

Arthur had had two wives, which was not previously known. The second, Guinevere, was buried in the same coffin, the bones being at his feet. And then he goes on to say: 'A tress of woman's hair, blond, and still fresh and bright in colour, was found in the coffin. One of the monks snatched it up and it immediately disintegrated into dust.'

Gerald of Wales commented on the size of the bones of Arthur's skeleton by saying that they were so big 'that in them the poet's words seem to be fulfilled:

'All men will exclaim at the size of the bones they've exhumed.' He continued: 'The abbot showed me one of the shin-bones. He held it upright on the ground against the foot of the tallest man he could find, and it stretched a good three inches above the man's knee. The skull was so large and capacious that it seemed a veritable prodigy of nature, for the space between the eyebrows and the eye-sockets was as broad as the palm of a man's hand. Ten or more wounds could clearly be seen, but they had all mended except one. This was larger than the others and it had made as immense gash. Apparently it was this wound which had caused Arthur's death.'

FAMOUS WRITERS IN ARTHURIAN COUNTRY

CHARLES DICKENS

As to your clambering, don't I know what happened of old? Don't I still see the Logan Stone, and you perched on the giddy top, while we, rocking it on its pivot, shrank from all that lay concealed below! Should I ever have blundered on the waterfall of St. Wighton, if you had not piloted the way? And when we got to Land's End, with the green sea far under us lapping into solitary rocky nooks where the mermaids live, who but you only had the courage to stretch over, to see those diamond jets of brightness that I swore then, and believe still, were the flappings of their tails! And don't I recall you again, sitting on the tip-top stone of the cradle turret over the highest battlement of the castle of St. Michael's Mount, with not a ledge or coign of vantage 'twixt you and the fathomless ocean under you, distant three thousand feet? Last, do I forget you clambering up the goat-path to King Arthur's Castle at Tintagel, when, in my vain wish to follow, I grovelled and clung to the soil like a caliban, and you, in the manner of a tricksy spirit and stout Ariel, actually danced up and down before me!

-from *The Life of Charles Dickens* by John Forster

ALGERNON SWINBURNE

Algernon Swinburne, the poet, visited Cornwall in 1864 when he wrote these extracts of letters to his favourite cousin, Mary Gordon, in the Isle of Wight. The poet lived at Bonchurch in the Undercliff, 1839-65:

> The sea-views are, of course, splendid beyond praise. On one headland (split now into two, divided by a steep isthmus of rock between two gulfs of sea, not wide enough for two to walk abreast across) is the double ruin, one half facing the other, of the old castle or palace of the Kings of Cornwall. Opposite on the high down is the old church, black with rain and time and storm, black at least in the tower, and grey in the body. The outer half of the castle, on the headland beyond the isthmus is on the very edge (and partly over the edge and on the slant) of the cliff, and has indescribable views of the double bay, broken cliffs, and outer sea. Practically, the *total* want of beach at any time of tide is a great loss."

As a result of his holidays in Cornwall, Swinburne later wrote his great poems, *Tristram of Lyonesse* and *A Tale of Balen* on Arthurian themes.

SWINBURNE

A letter (2 October,) also from Tintagel, gives an account of one of his seaside escapes:

> 'The aforesaid (a boy staying in the neighbourhood) came to see me, who have had an adventure which might have been serious but has only resulted in laming one foot for a day or two, I hope...... I had to run round a point of land which the sea was rising round, *or* be cut off in a bay of which to my cost I had just found the cliffs impracticable; so without boots or stockings I just ran at it and into the water and up or down over some awfully sharp and shell-encrusted rocks which cut my feet to fragments, had twice to plunge again into the sea, which was filling all the coves and swinging and swelling heavily between the rocks; once fell flat in it, and got so thrashed and licked that I might have been   in   's clutches (alluding to characters in a story), and at last got over the last reef and down on the sand of a safe bay, a drenched rag, and with feet that just took me home (three-quarters of a mile or so and uphill mainly with stones) half in and half out of the boots which I had just

saved with one hand; and then the right foot began to bleed like a pig, and I found a deep cut which was worse than any ever inflicted by a birch to the best of my belief, for it was *no end* bad yesterday, and to-day makes it hopeless to walk except on tiptoe, but as I wouldn't have it dressed or bothered I hope it will soon heal.'

In a later letter (October 26th) he says: "My foot is well enough now to be quite serviceable, and after full three weeks' close and often solitary confinement, I enjoy getting out among the downs and cliffs so much that I hardly know if I shall ever be able to tear myself away from my *last* chance of the sea this week."

THOMAS HARDY

Thomas Hardy, in 1870, was sent, in his capacity as architect, to restore the Cornish church of St Juliot, near Boscastle, where the vicar, Caddell Holder, had recently married for the second time, Helen Catherine Gifford. Her sister, Emma Lavinia Gifford, stayed with them as housekeeper. Hardy and Emma fell in love and were married in London on 17 September 1874. That first meeting at the vicarage of St Juliot inspired the poet to write 'When I set out for Lyonnesse' and the novel *A Pair of Blue Eyes.*

'When I Set Out for Lyonnesse'

When I set out for Lyonnesse,
   A hundred miles away,
   The rime was on the spray,
And starlight lit my lonesomeness
When I set out for Lyonnesse
   A hundred miles away.

What would bechance at Lyonnesse
   While I should sojourn there
   No prophet durst declare,
Nor did the wisest wizard guess
What would bechance at Lyonnesse
   When I should sojourn there.

When I came back from Lyonnesse
   With magic in my eyes,
   All marked with mute surmise
My radiance rare and fathomless,
When I came back from Lyonnesse
   With magic in my eyes!

After Emma's death Hardy wrote:
          'I Found Her Out There!

          I found her out there
     On a slope few see,
     That falls westwardly
     To the salt-edged air,
     Where the ocean breaks
     On the purple strand,
     And the hurricane shakes
     The solid land.

     I brought her here,
     And have laid her to rest
     In a noiseless nest
     No sea beats near.
     She will never be stirred
     In her loamy cell
     By the waves long heard
     And loved so well.

     So she does not sleep
     By those haunted heights
     The Atlantic smites
     And the blind gales sweep,
     Whence she often would gaze
     At Dundagel's famed head,
     While the dipping blaze
     Dyed her face fire-red;

     And would sigh at the tale
     Of sunk Lyonnesse,
     As a wind-tugged tress
     Flapped her cheek like a flail;
     Or listen at whiles
     With a thought-bound brow
     To the murmuring miles
     She is far from now.

     Yet her shade, maybe,
     Will creep underground

68

Tennyson Down where the poet walked with companions and composed many of his verses

Freshwater Bay and Tennyson Down, Isle of Wight

Victorian Windermere from Biskey Howe

St. Mary's, Isles of Scilly, Lyonesse.

Lands End - Lyonesse

Remnants of an ancient forest, Mounts Bay, Penzance, Cornwall - F.E. Gibson, St. Mary's, Scillies.

Slaughter Bridge, Camelford, the site of King Arthur's last fight.

Dozmary Pool, Bodmin Moor, Cornwall, where Bedivere threw Excalibur to the Lady of the Lake.

St. Michael's Tower, Glastonbury Tor

77

The Lady Chapel, Glastonbury Abbey, Somerset

SITE OF KING ARTHUR'S TOMB

Avalon - Arthur's Isle of Rest - at Glastonbury Tor. The tower is all that remains of St. Michael's chapel. Here Excalibur was said to have been forged and given magical qualities. 'Avalon' is supposedly derived from the Welsh 'Yns Avalion' meaning 'Island of Apples'; 'Glastonbury' is from 'Yorys Gutrin', from the Welsh 'Island of Glass' which the Saxons named Glastingebury.

Glastonbury Tor

Till it catch the sound
Of that western sea
As it swells and sobs
Where she once domiciled,
And joy in it throbs
With the heart of a child.

Hardy's *The Famous Tragedy of the Queen of Cornwall,* an Arthurian drama, was published and produced in 1923.

NOTES

THE GROWTH OF THE ARTHURIAN LEGEND

IN LITERATURE

Rolls Series - 'Chronicles and Memorials of Great Britain and Ireland from the Invasion of the Romans to the Reign of Henry VIII' (authorized 1857).

Tacitus: *The Agricola*

Caradoc of Llancarfan: *The Life of St. Gildas*

c.475-c. 515 Estimated birth and death of Arthur

Gildas: *De excidio et conquestu Britanniae.* Mentions battle of Mount Badon, but not Arthur, because he, allegedly, killed his own brother (*see* Gerald of Wales). He berated the Princes and clergy of his day for their violence and misdeeds. (c.548)

Aneirin: *Y Gododdin* (Welsh verse):- 'He glutted black ravens on the wall of the fort, although he was not Arthur.' (c.600)

Bede: *History of the English Church and People.* Derives his material from Gildas and the Annals. Fails to mention Arthur, but confirms there was a period of peace following the battle of Badon. A great scholar, Bede wrote more than 40 works, and although he was mostly at Jarrow monastery, his bones, after his death, were laid in Durham (673-735.)

Nennius: *Historia Brittonum.* Claimed Arthur had son, Anir, whom he killed and buried. Lived on border of Mercia in Brecknock or Radnor. Pupil of Elbod, bishop of Bangor (d. c.811). Four versions of *Historia,* it being a collection of notes on the history and geography of Britain. Describes Arthur as a *dux bellorum.* After Hengest's death, he claims, Arthur led Britons against Saxons, etc., in 12 victorious battles, including Badon. His history used by Geoffrey of Monmouth, and later Tennyson. (*fl.* 796).

Anglo-Saxon Chronicle. First portion to 892 written at King Alfred's behest. Compiled by monks at Winchester, Canterbury and Petersborough. Written from Anglo-Saxon viewpoint, Arthur is ignored. It is a chronological record of British history from the time of Christ to mid-12c.

Annales Cambriae. Ancient annals of Wales, of which earliest record extant dates from the second half of the tenth century. Refer to battle of Badon 'in which Arthur carried the cross of our Lord Jesus Christ on his shoulder (shield), and the British were victors'. Also refers to 'strife of Camlann' in 539, in which Arthur and Medrant (Mordred) fell. (C.10)

William of Malmesbury: *Gesta Regum Anglorum* (c.1125). Arthur mentioned, and he calls him 'a man clearly worthy to be proclaimed in true histories.' He was educated at Malmesbury Abbey, where he was librarian. Revised *Gesta Historia Novella* (to 1142); *Gesta Pontificum Anglorum* (to 1125); and *De Antiquitate Glastoniensibus Ecclesiae* (written 1129-1139)

BRITISH

Geoffrey of Monmouth: *History of the Kings of England* (c.1090-1143). This is the chief source of historical evidence on Arthur, derived from Nennius; but is unreliable. Tennyson used it as source material. Geoffrey writes enthusiastically of Arthur's life and times incorporated in one chapter. (c.1136)

Layamon: *Brut.* 'Layamon' meant *Law man.* A priest of Ernley Arley Regis, Worcester, his history, *Brut,* covered the period from the legendary arrival of Brutus to Cadwallader (689). It was based on Wace's French version of *Historia Regum Britanniae* by Geoffrey of Monmouth. There were additional Norman and Breton sources, but wrote story of Arthur in English. Also wrote on Lear and Cymbeline. The alliteration of the verse is frequently abandoned and replaced by rhyme. Tennyson's source material. (c.1200)

Black Book of Carmarthen: a poem in Welsh (MS 12C.) containing a collection of ancient Welsh poetry referring to Arthur (1312? -69).

Welsh: The Mabinogion, (Culhwch and Olwen, Rhonabwy's dream preserve independent Welsh tradition; *Gereint, Owein* and *Peredur* use stories also handled by Chrétien).

Gerald of Wales: *The Journey through Wales* and *The Description of Wales.* There are several references to Arthur and the two Merlins. He reports the reason why Gildas never mentioned Arthur. There are two long passages in *De Principis Instructione* and *Speculum Ecclesiae* discussing the discovery at Glastonbury of Arthur's tomb and how it was identified. According to Gerald Arthur conferred many gifts and favours on Glastonbury monastery during his lifetime. (1188)

Adam of Domerham: *Historia de Rebus Gestis Glastoniensibus* (*see* Gerald of Wales). Said Arthur's body had lain in tomb at Glastonbury for 648 years.

Starting from G. of Monmouth's date of 542 for the Battle of Camlann, this dates his exhumation at 1191.

Robert of Gloucester: Reputed author of the *Metrical Chronicles* to 1272. Personal reminiscences in long lines rhyming to 14 syllables and more. These are the work of many hands assuredly, composed in the Abbey of Gloucester. In them a description of Oxford in 1263 and the death of Simon de Montford of Evesham.

Geoffrey Chaucer: 'The Wife of Bath's Tale,' an allegory from *The Canterbury Tales*. A bawdy story of a knight of the Round Table who raped a girl. The Court condemned him to death. Alternatively, he had to find the answer to what women most desired, within a year and a day. Failure to do so, he would still be executed. Needless to say the Knight found the right answer. Written in blank verse. (1392-4)

Sir Gawain and the Green Knight, The Ballad of Tarn Wadling (an alliterative poem in 2 parts) and *Morte Arthure* are three poems of unknown authorship. Finest of them is the first of more than 2,500 lines, alliterative, and in four Fits, cantos or sections. In it the gallant and good Knight Gawain beheads the Green Knight, who represents Satan or evil, who nevertheless challenges him to a further duel after Gawain has undergone several trials and temptations. Gawain passes the tests and survives another encounter with the Green Knight.

FRENCH AND GERMAN

Geoffrey Gaimar: *L'Estoire des Engles*. Translated Geoffrey's history into French verse.

Wace of Jersey: *Roman de Brut* and *Gestedes Normandes*. French verse chronicle dedicated to Eleanor of Aquitaine. It included much of Geoffrey's information up to her reign from Constantine onwards. First to introduce the Round Table. Layamon adapted this in a translation (first long poem in English). Tennyson's source material.

Marie de France: *Lais*, which Chrétien de Troyes developed in *Matière de Bretagne*, the Arthurian story; then taken up by Robert de Boron. Abbess of Shaftesbury (1181-1215)

Robert de Boron: *Joseph D' Arimathea, Merlin* and *Perceval*. A French poet, in his trilogy the story of the Holy Grail is developed, associating it with

Arthur. Only the first and second parts survive of these poems. (c.1190 and 1201-2)

Chrétien de Troyes: *Arthurian Romances Enide,* c.1170; *Cliges,* c.1176 *Yvain* and *Lancelot* (unfinished), 1177-81. Perceval, 1181-(unfinished).
The Vulgate Cycle: c. 1215-30. Made up of 5 separate works:
i) *L'Estoire del Saint Graal,* ii) *the Vulgate Merlin,* iii) *the 'Lancelot* proper.' iv) *La Queste del Saint Graal* v) *La Mort le Roi Artu.* These works combine unity of plan with an apparent variety of authors. The 2 first romances were added subsequently to the last 3, the 'Prose Lancelot' which were clearly planned as a whole, though written by different authors. The *Estoire* draws on Robert de Boron's *Joseph of Arimathea* and other material linking the Grail to the Arthurian world; the *Vulgate Merlin* is a prose reworking of Robert's *Merlin* with pseudo-historical material on the rise of Arthur added.

Béroul *The Romance of Tristan* (c.1200)
Other possible sources of legend were Eilhart von Oberg or Thomas d'Angleterre.
Thomas Chestre: *Sir Launfal,* a poem about a Knight of the Round Table. He leaves Court offended by the misconduct of Guinevere, Arthur's wife. Lives in poverty at Caerleon. The story occurs in *Lais* by Marie de France (12C.)

German:
Gottfried von Strassburg: *Tristan* (c.1210)
Thomas: Tristan (c.1160)
Wolfram von Eschenbach: *Parzival* (c.1200-10)

ARTHUR FROM MIDDLE AGES TO T. HARDY

Robert W. Ackerman, writing in *Arthurian Literature in the Middle Ages* (ed. R.S. Loomis), lists Arthurian tales written in the Middle English period:

Arthur and Merlin (1250-1300)
Sir Tristrem (c.1300)
Libeaus Desconus (pre-1340)
Sir Perceval of Galles (pre-1340)
Sir Launfal (pre-1340)
Ywain and Gawain (c.1350)
Arthur (1350-1400)
Chaucer's *Wife of Bath's Tale* (1392-4)
The Stanzaic *Morte Arthur* (c.1400)

The Carl of Carlisle (c.1400)
The Avowing of King Arthur (c.1425)
Lovelich's *Holy Grail and Merlin* (c.1430)
The Gest of Sir Gawain (c.1450)
The Wedding of Sir Gawain (c.1450)
Prose *Merlin* (c.1450)
Lancelot of the Laik (1482-1500)
Malory's *Le Morte d'Arthur* (1485)
King Arthur's Death (c.1500)
The Green Knight (c.1500)
The Turk and Gawain (c.1500)
Prose *Joseph of Arimathea* (early 16th century)
King Arthur and King Cornwall (early 16th century)
The Boy and the Mantle (16th century)

Poetry from Edmund Spenser to Thomas Hardy:

Edmund Spenser: (1552?-99) *The Faery Queen.*
Wm. Camden: (1551-1623) *Britannia.*
Michael Drayton: (1563-1631) *Polyolbion* (1622).
John Milton: (1608-74) *The History of Britain, Paradise Regained, Lycidas.*
John Dryden: (1631-1700) *King Arthur, or the British Worthy* (opera, 1691).
Sir Walter Scott: (1771-1832) *The Bridal of Triermain,* etc.
Wm. Wordsworth: (1770-1850) *Artegal and Elidure, The Egyptian Maid.*
R.S. Hawker: (1803-75) *The Quest of the Sangraal.* (1864)
Alfred Tennyson: (1809-1892) pre-*Idyll* lyrics, *Idylls of the King, Merlin and the Gleam* (1889).
Matthew Arnold: (1822-88) *Tristram and Iseult.*
Wm. Morris: (1834-96) *Defence of Guinevere.*
Algernon Swinburne: (1837-1909) *Tristram of Lyonesse.*
Thos. Hardy: (1840-1928) *Queen of Cornwall, When I Set out for Lyonesse,* etc.

The 1842 Arthurian Lyrics of Tennyson

1.   *The Lady of Shalott:* published 1832; from the Italian novelette *Donna* di Scalotta. Revised poem in 1842; transformed into Elaine in the *Idylls of the King,* and there based on Malory's work, *Le Morte d'Arthur,* 1485.
2.   *Sir Galahad:* published 1834 as a male counterpart to *St Agnes' Eve.* Evolved into *The Holy Grail* of the *Idylls.* Published also in 1842.
3.   *Sir Lancelot and Queen Guinevere:* published in 1842, but partly written in 1830. It was intended as companion-poem for *Shalott.*
4.   *The Epic* (prefatory to *Morte d'Arthur):* published in 1842, but written about 1837/8.

5. *Morte d'Arthur:* published 1842, but written in 1833/4 on receiving news of the death of his intimate friend, Arthur Henry Hallam in 1833. The poem was expanded in *The Idylls of the King* and published as *The Passing of Arthur,* 1869. Sources predominantly Malory, Nennius, Geoffrey of Monmouth and the French romances.

Sources of Tennyson's Arthur

The Idylls of the King: by Alfred Lord Tennyson
    For the convenience of readers the sources and publication dates of the twelve *Idylls of the King* are listed below:

1. *The Coming of Arthur:* Published 1869; Malory i, Layamon and Geoffrey of Monmouth's *History of the Kings of Britain,* Nennius, Gildas, & Welsh Annals.
2. *Gareth and Lynette:* published 1872; Malory vii.
3. *The Marriage of Geraint:* published 1859; Mabinogion *(Geraint, son of Erbin,* translated by Lady Charlotte Guest, and *Erec and Enid,* by Chrétien de Troyes.)
4. *Geraint and Enid:* published 1859; *Mabinogion.*
5. *Balin and Balan:* published 1885; Malory ii partly. Mostly original.
6. *Merlin and Vivien:* published 1859; Malory iv an i.
7. *Lancelot and Elaine;* published 1870; Malory xviii and Nennius.
8. *The Holy Grail:* published 1869 (cp. *Sir Galahad);* Malory xiii, xi, xvii, xiv, xii, xvi.
9. *Pelleas and Ettarre:* published 1869; Malory iv.
10. *The Last Tournament:* published 1872; Malory viii and x.
11. *Guinevere:* published 1859; Malory xxi and xx.
12. *The Passing of Arthur:* (expanded from *Morte d'Arthur)* published 1869; Malory xxi, Geoffrey of Monmouth's *History* and *The Death of King Arthur.*
Merlin and The Gleam: published 1889. cp. *Merlin and Nimue* in the *Idylls* in which Nimue means the 'Gleam' - that is, the *higher poetic imagination.*

FURTHER READING

Arthurian Literature in the Middle Ages, ed. R.S. Loomis. OUP. 1959.
The Cambridge Book of Prose & Verse - to the Cycles of Romances, Ed. Sampson. CUP. 1924.
King Arthur's Avalon, ed. Geoffrey Ashe. Collins, 1957.
King Arthur & the Grail, Richard Cavendish. Paladin. 1978.
The Age of Arthur (3 vols.), gen. ed. John Morris. Phillimore.
History from the Sources: Gildas, Nennius & St Patrick (3 vols.), gen. ed. John Morris, Phillimore.
Arthur's Britain, Leslie Alcock. Penguin Books. 1973.

The Quest for Arthur's Britain, ed. Geoffrey Ashe. Paladin. 1971.

Anthologies

The Earliest English Poems, ed. Michael Alexander. Penguins. 1966.
Oxford Book of Welsh Verse in English, ed. Gwyn Jones. OUP. 1977.
A Celtic Miscellany, ed. Kenneth Jackson. Penguins. 1951.

Arthurian Literature

The Death of King Arthur; translated by James Cable (Penguins)
Sir Gawain & the Green Knight; translated by Brian Stone (Penguins)
Tristan, Gottfried von Strassburg; translated by M.A.T. Hatto (Penguins)
The Mabinogion; translated by Jeffrey Gantz (Penguins)
The Romance of Tristan. Béroul; translated by S. Fedrick (Penguins)
The Quest of the Holy Grail; translated by P.M. Matarasso (Penguins)
Arthurian Chronicles, Wace & Layamon; translated by Engene Mason and Gwyn Jones (Dents Everyman)
The Journey Through Wales & The Description of Wales, Gerald of Wales; translated by Lewis Thorpe (Penguins)
The History of the Kings of Britain, Geoffrey of Monmouth; translated by Lewis Thorpe (Penguins)
Le Morte d'Arthur, Sir Thomas Malory; edited by Janet Cowen & introduction by John Lawlor (Penguins)
Idylls of the King, Alfred Lord Tennyson; edited by Christopher Ricks (Longmans)

For catalogue of furtherbooks of Cornish interest
send to:
Dyllansow Truran
  Trewolsta
    Trewirgie
      Redruth
        Cornwall